STAR
IN
THE SHED
WINDOW

STAR IN THE SHED WINDOW

Collected Poems
1933–1988

James Hayford

The New England Press
Shelburne, Vermont

Hayford, James
    Star in the shed window : collected poems / by James Hayford. —
1st ed.
        p. cm.
        Includes index.
        ISBN 0-933050-66-6   — ISBN 0-933050-74-7 (pbk.)
        I. Title.
PS3558.A84S74 1989
811'.54—dc20   89-9279
                                                    CIP
    Acknowledgment is made to the editors of the following publications in which some of
these poems first appeared: *Harper's, Saturday Evening Post, The New Yorker, Ladies Home
Journal, Massachusetts Review, Vermonter, Counter/Measures,* and *Green Mountains Review.*
    Five of the poems first appeared in *New Poems by American Poets #2,* Rolfe Humphries,
Editor; New York, 1957.
    Four of the poems first appeared as *Four Women,* Janus Press, Claire Van Vliet, 1981.

For additional copies or for a catalog of our other New England titles,
please write:

    The New England Press
    P.O. Box 575
    Shelburne, VT 05482

for Helen

Star in the Shed Window

Coming into the shed without a light,
I saw the window blue with the outside night,
And in an upper pane a star to keep
My silhouetted sawhorse and my ax:
Observatories in the merest shacks
Open upon the universal deep.

1936

Contents

Preface

To Learn to Swim

My father used to maintain with a perfectly straight face that the way to teach a boy to swim was to throw him in deep water and walk away. This was the way he had taught his dog Smut to swim. Smut was a success.

The theory seemed to be, if a kid was worth saving, he'd save himself.

He didn't actually apply this educational theory to me—my mother wouldn't let him. He just kept telling me this was what *ought* to be done, while holding me across his arms face down in the Atlantic Ocean and ordering me to thrash around. Of course it took a lot of breath to thrash as vigorously as he demanded, and every time I breathed I got a lungful of salt water. I was not a success. This may have been partly because my mother stood nearby in the water up to her shins, which was about as far in as she ever got, saying, "Oh—Floyd—*don't!*" She always explained that she was afraid of water, and so, after two or three minutes, was I.

I shall carry this fear till I die. Not that I never learned to swim. I had to in order to graduate from Amherst College. So many educated men were drowning that the smarter colleges had begun including in their degree requirements "the ability to swim a hundred yards." It took me two whole shivering winters in that cold, highly chlorinated college pool, but Tug Kennedy, the swimming coach, saw to it that I made it. A big, gentle man, he used occasionally to pick me up and slide me into the deep end head first in a vain attempt to add diving to my accomplishments. In this he failed. Or rather, I failed.

Swimming has since then been my favorite sport—in fact, my only sport. But I'm still careful never to go out very far beyond where I can touch bottom. And I wade in. It may be that my failure to master the water element in my life is the source of some of my other fears.

You can see by now why I'm concerned about this failure—why I was so concerned about teaching my son that I wrote a poem about it. He did not fail, but became a strong, fearless swimmer—no particular thanks to me: he learned at a summer boys' camp.

While Tug was throwing me bodily into the pool, Robert Frost, in his house on Sunset Avenue on the other side of town, was throwing me mentally, in our visits every now and then, into the perilous seas of literature. (Amherst was some town.) Both places, it was sink or swim—as my father had known to begin with.

To Learn To Swim

Let the child learn to swim
Where it's too deep for him
To touch his toes to sand:
Let him right then begin
To *be* in when he's in
By doing without land.

Let him for his own sake
Require himself to make
It from the end of the dock
Out to the diving float,
Or further out, to a boat
Or some deep-water rock—

Keeping his head and breath
While buoyed by certain death.

Mr. Frost had stopped giving courses by the time I entered Amherst. However, he was still serving as poet in residence; this meant that he was available to talk with interested individuals or groups. The English Honors men, of whom I was later one, went annually to spend an evening at his house.

My first meeting with him was set up by my great Shakespeare teacher, Theodore Baird. I showed Baird a poem I had written, and he said why didn't I consult a real expert.

In view of the fact that I was a Vermont boy with a literary bent, it seems odd that I hadn't been introduced to Frost's work until that very fall—the fall of my sophomore year (1932). For my birthday in October, my parents sent me a copy of his *Collected Poems* of 1930. I found this first taste so exciting that for two weeks or more I could hardly put the book down to go to classes. I read the poems over and over. At Montpelier High School I had had a fine English teacher, Harriet Knight, who introduced me to many poets. Keats and Tennyson were my favorites; in their magic countries I lost myself for a while. In Frost's book I found myself. This was my country; these were my people, my ways of thinking and feeling, my tones of voice.

I approached this great man with awe.

He began by visiting with me about Vermont. He was still living at South Shaftsbury when he was not at Amherst, and he had noticed that I was the only Vermonter in the college that year. The only other Vermonter.

He said he understood I had a poem to show him. He read it silently, laid it down, leaned back in his chair, and began talking—about everything in general, it seemed. It was fascinating talk, full of surprising turns and amusing stories. All I had to do was nod when he looked at me, or say "I see" when he paused. He didn't seem to be talking about the poem at all. Not that I minded; it was great fun listening. When Mrs. Frost appeared, he introduced me. She said, "Rob, supper's ready." I got up and started for the door. But he wasn't through yet; I stood with my hand on the doorknob for half an hour.

One thing that he said I remember clearly. He said, "I tell you the opposite of what I tell most college poets. They don't have much to say, but they say it very well. You have something to say, but you don't say it very well."

On my way back to the dorm in the dark, I began tracing the main thread back through his monologue. It came to me, piece by piece, how everything he had said, or as much of it as I could remember, applied to the poem, or to me. When he talked, everything he said reminded him of something else. Every consideration led to a further consideration. He had simply been putting my poem in its setting, as he saw it—an infinitely rich and complex setting. I had been given the product of his years of reading and thinking. And writing. And talking.

The next spring, I got a phone call in the dormitory: "Mr. Hayford? This is Frost. I'm leaving for Shaftsbury for the summer, and I called to say good-bye. Come see me again in the fall." I did, and several times more.

At graduation time, in 1935, my class asked me to be the Ivy Poet. Just as I started to read my longish poem to the crowd on the lawn beside Johnson Chapel, I saw Mr. Frost and Stanley King, president of Amherst, slide into a couple of front-row seats. The poem, called "Music and Poetry," recounted a young man's struggle to decide whether to spend his life in music or in poetry; he chose poetry.

Next day, at the Alumni Luncheon in the Baseball Cage, at which grad-
uating seniors were guests, President King, after awarding the customary
honors, paused, and announced that a new fellowship was to be established
in honor of Robert Frost. Its first recipient was to be yesterday's Ivy Poet—
I wondered whether to trust my ears. Applause broke out. I dragged the
sleeve of my new white linen jacket through my pink ice cream as I rose
to acknowledge it. I stood trying to contain the drip with my paper napkin.
Beside me smiled my father, who had had a non-swimmer on his hands
all those years—his only child, he who had been captain of his high school
football, basketball, and baseball teams—he who had had to go to work
to help support his family after only one year of high school.

In *A Swinger of Birches*, his book about Frost, Sidney Cox gives this
account of the Fellowship:

> One commencement, near the end of Robert Frost's
> second hitch at Amherst, President King was apparently
> pleased with what Robert Frost had said in his address—or
> with the state of mind just then of his trustees—for the Pres-
> ident said to the poet that he would like him to ask for an
> administrative favor.
>
> "Even to the half of thy kingdom?" Robert said.
>
> "Even to the half of my kingdom," President King smil-
> ingly replied.
>
> Robert asked for a scholarship to be given to a student
> of his selection, according to provisions that he set. The pres-
> ident agreed. And Robert selected the boy who had shown
> the most power of making up his own mind, and stipulated
> that he should "go somewhere in the United States," take
> no courses, seek no guidance, and produce something to suit
> himself. Neither project nor production had to be submit-
> ted. He was to be terrifyingly on his own. (Sidney Cox, *A
> Swinger of Birches* [New York: New York University Press,
> 1957], 66-67).

When I went up to Mr. Frost after the Alumni Luncheon to thank
him—rather stammeringly—I had had absolutely no inkling that anything
like this was in the wind—he said, in his best mock-stern manner, "There
are some terrible conditions attached to this. You're going to have to worry
about 'em all night. Come see me tomorrow afternoon."

These were the dread conditions. I was to:

Receive $1,000 (perhaps like $10,000 now);
Stay away from graduate schools, art colonies, big cities, and Europe;
Produce a book of poems in twenty years;
Be terrifyingly on my own.

He told me that he and I were going to call the Fellowship the Desert or Bo Tree Fellowship. I was to go live in the Desert; I was to go sit under a Bo Tree, as did the Buddha. Of course everybody else called it the Robert Frost Fellowship.

As for staying away from Europe, my roommate Jim Miller (James W. Miller, later president of Western Michigan University) and I had signed up for a summer at the University of Heidelberg. This was 1935; Hitler desperately needed American tourists, so we got a good deal. Mr. Frost agreed to grant me this exception to his rule.

What Frost wanted the Fellowship to do was to spare its holder the necessity, at least for a while, of taking more degrees; to prevent his getting mixed up with literary cliques; and to save him from winding up as a professor, a critic, or an expatriate—in short, to save him for American poetry. The twenty-year part of it harked back to what Frost said to his grandfather when the latter gave him a farm and a year to make good writing poetry on it. Frost said, "Give me twenty! Give me twenty!"—like an auctioneer.

I left Amherst a free, exalted, and dedicated young man. I didn't see how it could possibly take me twenty years.

Jim Miller and I sailed for Germany a few days later, along with about ten other male graduates and undergraduates, chiefly from Amherst, and about ten young women, chiefly from Vassar. We spent a very sociable summer in each other's company.

I had never had much interest in politics, but the outward signs of what the Nazis were doing to Germany made me sit up and take notice—when I wasn't thinking about my awesome future responsibilities and what Mr. Frost expected of me.

Before starting for home, I sailed to England by myself, and spent a memorable week in Salisbury (my first Norman cathedral), Winchester (my first Gothic one), Oxford (I saw a lock of Milton's hair), and London (a production of *A Midsummer Night's Dream* in Regent's Park at night).

Montpelier, Vermont, seemed as eligible a place as any for me to settle in, considering all the places that were forbidden, so I returned to my parents' home there.

At Christmas, my cousin Helen Emerson, whom I had known since childhood, came to visit us. She and I fell in love and decided to get married. Consanguinity was a consideration, but my family doctor said that since there was no history of insanity or other abnormality on either side, our chances of having normal children were pretty good.

President King is said to have objected to Mr. Frost that marriage wasn't included in the terms of the Fellowship, and Mr. Frost is said to have replied that marriage was among the few things that weren't excluded.

Mr. Frost wrote to me:

> I don't suppose we can either of us expect to have as good a time again with that fellowship as we both had that day of its first award . . . I shall probably never be as sure again of my choice for the appointment. My safest way is not to think of it too hard, just as yours is not to try to profit too much. Easy does it for both of us.

I am still wondering which meaning he intended in that second sentence: "I shall probably never be as sure again of my choice for the appointment." Did he mean he would never be as sure about somebody else for a future appointment? Or, that he would never be as sure again about me? I hoped he meant the former, of course, but felt bound to keep the latter in mind. Frost was not a man to waste his ambiguities on the desert air.

The plain fact is that the Fellowship was never again awarded. And herein lies, of course, a further ambiguity: was I such an outstanding success that he couldn't hope to match me? Or such a dismal disappointment that he couldn't bear to risk a repeat? Or neither of the above?

Of course I did try to profit too much. I wrote some long, portentous poems in an oratorical style. He urged me, in visits and by letter: Talk—let me hear voice-tones.

But when I tried to talk in poetry, I sounded exactly like him. I admired him so much, and thought all his poetic theories were so right . . .

He was patient with me. I simply wasn't old enough or wise enough to see that he had in effect put all New England under his copyright, for poetic purposes, and that anyone who rashly undertook to grow in his immense shadow was bound to have a thin time of it, despite occasional encouraging words from him. It was going to take me some years to learn how to be original while treating his kind of material in what seemed the only sensible way—very much his kind of way.

"You are going to get the fusion of your elements," he wrote me. I lived on that sentence for two or three years—on that sentence and what little I could earn giving piano lessons for twenty-five cents each and serving as local organist and choirmaster for three dollars a week. We had a son, and the thousand dollars was soon gone. Helen's mother helped us with food; my parents helped us with money.

For a person with no experience, school-teaching jobs were hard to get in those Depression years. I finally landed one, teaching English at Goddard Junior College in Barre. One year later I helped transform it into the "progressive" Goddard College in Plainfield.

In discouragement I gave up writing poetry altogether, and wrote novels, stories, plays—all pretty bad. I wrote a few educational articles that were published, and a revolutionary grammar text that almost was.

I got a Master's degree in the teaching of English and history at Columbia University. My essay was on Frost; I took a perverse delight in pointing out his limitations. This desperate act finally emancipated me. I'm sure he never saw the wretched thing.

After two years of teaching junior high school history and English in New Jersey, I fled back to Vermont and taught history for four years at Burr and Burton Seminary in Manchester. During this time I managed to place a few poems in a few good magazines: *Harper's*, *Saturday Evening Post*, *The New Yorker*.

Early in 1948 former vice-president Henry Wallace announced his candidacy for president on a third-party ticket, calling for negotiations with the Soviet Union to end the Cold War and head off a ruinous rivalry in nuclear weapons. This made sense to me, and I joined with other Vermonters to back him. The American Communist Party also decided to back Wallace instead of putting up a candidate of their own. Consequently all of his backers were accused of having Communist sympathies. I resigned from Burr and Burton when my support of Wallace became a controversial issue. I was one of the Vermont delegates to the convention in Philadelphia where we founded the Progressive Party and nominated Wallace. The FBI was there, getting us all on film. Vermont's most influential newspaper kept calling on us Progressives, by name, to go back to Russia where we belonged.

Certainly in this atmosphere of feverish anti-communism, no school in the state was going to touch me with a ten-foot pole. I withdrew to West Burke, Vermont, where Helen's brother had a house for sale, bought four milk goats and six hens and became a small farmer. I started a novel, took on a few piano pupils, and edited textbooks for a Columbia Teachers College professor whose student I had recently been.

And all of a sudden the poetry came back with a rush. Farming agreed with me. I remember the day in our kitchen in West Burke when I first realized I was hearing *my own voice* speaking in a poem. Perhaps I had actually been hearing it off and on for some time, but I hadn't become aware of it. I walked around the house for the rest of the day, saying those lines over and over, listening to myself.

In 1954, when Helen and I made our annual summer visit to Mr. Frost in his cabin near Bread Loaf, he read a poem I had brought him, looked up—and said what I'd waited years to hear. He started, "Now, I wouldn't say this the way you do—" He broke off. "But I have to remember you go at things your way. Your way isn't like mine. You've found your own way. You've found your own voice."

It had taken only nineteen years.

A word should be said about the methods I have used in dating and arranging the poems in this book.

They are dated by the year in which they first appear—or their beginnings first appear—in my journals. In many cases the beginnings are quite unpromising. Some start out in a wholly different direction from the one they finally take. I say "finally" with tongue in cheek, because I have learned never to be sure that a poem has stopped developing. I say it to myself or to someone else—sometimes to an audience—and discover to my dismay that it doesn't quite say what it means to say. Perhaps some minor emphasis in it works against the major emphasis. Perhaps it's simply clumsy. Anyway, something about it doesn't work. So I revise it, very carefully now, after years of making revisions that eliminated one fault but introduced another—revisions that did as much harm as good. I now lay it out in all its possible variations, tenderly preserving whatever quality it may have, making sure to enhance and brighten rather than diminish or dim, determining that the whole thing now hangs together and reads as though it had just sprung newborn and fully developed from my fertile brain—and lay it aside for six months. When I revisit it, it either works or does not work. In the latter case, I try again. All I can say for sure is that all the poems in this book are as good as I can make them right now.

This means that whenever in the past I have published a collection I have included, naturally, poems that were new at the time, and also, perhaps less naturally, older poems, some previously collected, some not, that had recently been revised. Don't be surprised, then, to find a poem dated 1941, for example, between a poem dated 1984 and a poem dated 1962.

You may draw the conclusion that few of my poems have shaped up easily. Almost every one has been sweated over; a few have been agonized over. Every poem in this book, however light or carefree it may sound, represents a serious attempt to say something, and a more or less difficult struggle to get it right.

My perhaps curious methods of work and of publication have had one equally curious side-effect: they have given my product a certain kind of consistency or uniformity. The poems do not readily divide into early, middle, and late, as far as style is concerned. Many if not most of them have been worked on fairly recently. Thus the periods of my life are reflected in subject matter more than in style. For example, it will be evident that my farming years were from 1948 to 1954.

Living mainly in Vermont villages and towns, I have paid considerable attention to the comings and goings of the seasons. Many of the poems show this preoccupation—so many, in fact, that from my first collection I have tended to arrange them in accordance with the seasonal flow, tucking the ones that have no seasonal connotation into the intervals between seasons, as it were.

This makes for variety—an ever-shifting scene—and also for a certain impression of confusion, until you catch on to my informal principles of organization.

In the end, of course, each poem remains a separate entity, and where it occurs in the apparent order or disorder is in most cases immaterial. In this, a book of poem̶ ̶ ̶ ̶ ̶ a box of chocolates: it doesn't matter what order you ̶ ̶ ̶ ̶ ̶ ̶ ̶ pétit.

The Equivocal Sky

The Waves

The green waves mount, crash coolly, turn, and run.
Their glints are old and new under the sun.
The timeless and the temporary are one.

In the emptiness of their uneasy pause
I hear myself recollecting who I was—
Identity, my papers, my lost cause.

1943

The Never-Last Outpost

Leaving the last outlying farm,
North for an hour through cedar swamp,
You may well come to a square made calm
And civil by the old plain pomp

Of elms drawn up on either hand,
Where a slender church reproves excess,
And a fiddle shapes a saraband
Against the immediate wilderness.

1938

Hard Water

These hard, sleek pebbles of the brook
Are the soul of water as a book
May be the soul of man: they hold
In permanent miniature the cold,
The impersonal, the wave, the fish—
Take one to pocket if you wish.

1942

Business Obligation

World where ambitious men
Tread on each other's heels,
I can remember when
You taught me how failure feels.

Yet if a man resign
The world, he may repent,
And loneliness is a sign
Of self-imprisonment.

Tranquil to do my work
In neighborly isolation
Is to accept, not shirk,
My business obligation.

1949

Strength in a Testing

Let winter fall severe
On the late war's survivors,
Or fortune blank and queer
Forsake sincere believers,
Watchers grow weak with fear.

Watchers are apt to doubt
Their own strength in a testing,
And nothing frays strength out
Like this uneasy resting
In front of every bout.

Those in the thick of it
Are too busy staying alive
To dread another hit,
Too proud of being brave
To wish they were fortunate.

1949

Without Intrusion

Its lampflame's soft suffusion
Invites me as I pass
To read without intrusion
Its life behind the glass,

This stark and lonely shack
Bowered in the meadow's crease,
Abandoned a while back,
Well set for crime, or peace.

Someone is there this winter,
Content or cursing squalor,
As owner or as renter
Bespeaking no strange caller.

1950

The Afternoons Before Christmas

Don't let it fool you at this season
When in defiance of all reason
Strange happenings occupy the air
In room and street and everywhere.

Old enemies are offering truce—
Miss Spence even waves to Mrs. Luce—
Or are these optical illusions?
Don't let them lead you to conclusions.

The sun looks warmer than it feels,
And every autumn as it wheels
Further and further off, the town
Is lost if heaven does not come down.

1943

The Light on the Mountain

Their light's no more than a spark
Under the mountain's head,
But when they go to bed
They leave the country dark.

What time is it? Not late—
The night is not far gone:
Forerunners of the dawn
Are in their beds by eight.

And all they prophesy
Is that cold light will break,
And country stretch and wake
To an equivocal sky.

1950

The Winter Lamb

Hush now, have you not heard?
Born to the cutting cold,
The winter lamb comes furred—
A white ball slickly rolled,
Well-snouted, dour, absurd.
There in the littered fold
Its first unmuffled word
Is clamorous and bold—
Sleep easy, now you've heard.

1950

Good Friday Noon

With heads fittingly bowed
We walked to Christ Church, mother and I,

But I, less grave than proud,
Went with delighted downcast eye

Because at last allowed
To go in bare shoes where it was dry.

1933

The Headstrong Sun

Inflamed, the headstrong sun
Surmounts the leaf-clad earth
Who circles him in passion
To bring her seed to birth.

What if a cloud's intrusion
Interrupt them in their noon—
We feel her sudden shiver
Along the mottled river—

Let what he drew from water
Thwart his perspiring eye:
He will but pore the hotter
And blot the streambed dry.

1949

7

Circular

Of all wrong things the wrongest,
Surely, is to lament
Because the sun's descent
Dates from the day he's strongest—
Summer's first day is longest:

Among smart men the smartest
Is still the provident artist
Whose business is to know,
Even before the snow,
Winter's first day is shortest.

Fact and anticipation,
Alternate currents of joy,
Await our free employ
In this subsolar station
Where all is circulation.

1950

Both Ways of Winning

In each divided inning
You take both ways of winning:

Conservative in the field—
How little can you yield?

But then at bat, let's go—
Let's spoil the status quo!

You want to be wild *and* tame
To win the national game.

1949

8

Forecast Tonight

Forecast tonight are fog and rain—
The rain begins. Our roof is tight
Except for one small place in the porch
Which will not worry us: we're all right.

Luxuriously we have two thousand
Square feet over us three and the cat;
The goats and pullets in the barn
Share their six hundred—no leaks in that.

But our thoughts now are out the window
Of our upstairs bedroom in Vermont
Where the radiance of our lamp is quenched
In dripping black: may none be in want.

Co-dwellers all along this seaboard,
Are your roofs sound, each several one,
Millions in all, as we come under
The common rain in unison?

1948

Country Content

Under these sober skies
Blunt hills and sharp roofs rise.
The hills confine the sight,
The rooftops are the height
At which the workings of
The heart are halted: love
Must be held in and down—
So says the country town.

The country is content.
(The city's different.)
The corn and cattle grow,
Men plod and rivers flow.
Under the gabled roofs
They go on finding proofs
That love of things and the past
Is the only love at last.

Flat clouds and tilted land.
Trust what you can take in hand.
Things and the past are pleasant.
As for people, and the present . . .

1942

Elm and Apple

The land is lovelier for trees
That keep their figures lithe
By being blithe
And dancing with each passing breeze—

And also for the sober stock
That branch close to the root
To bear us fruit,
And crook their elbows against shock.

1936

Starting a Poem

Infuse the hour you snatch
With courtesy to man
And the whole shooting match:

Courtesy really can
Help a misgiving hatch
Into a working plan.

1950

Style

As the cold currents of the brook
Render its sands and pebbles clear,
Just so does style in man or book
Brighten the content, bring it near.

1950

To Poets

Though much we do is done for us
By spirit or spirits anonymous
Who when received find avenue
To things we had not known we knew,
Still, most will be by our own hand
As we keep answering the demand
Of good in people and the land.

1950

Playing Fields

From testing your intelligence
At poetry or farming
You shift the event to ground less tense
Where error's not alarming:

At checkers depth is your defense
By tactics quaint and charming
On a board both intimate and immense
With red and black men swarming;

The keyboard too has its extents
Where fingers find it calming
To trace once more the soft descents
Of sequences disarming.

1950

Parental

What will befall you now
Is out of my control—
What wars you fight in, how
You save your soul.

Though still I intervene
From sympathy or anger,
My presence on the scene
Won't spoil your danger.

1949

To the Float

To the float is only a hundred yards,
But dusk is making it look dimmer;
And see, no guards—
The two of us, no other swimmer.

True, one should trust it under one,
This cooling sheet of cobalt shimmer—
So cool a son!
I'll swim you out where the camplights glimmer.

1949

Not Yet

The further on you get
The more you cry Not yet,
Not yet—a little while
That I may reconcile

The world my creditor;
One time I blamed him for
Granting no larger loan,
And now I would atone.

1950

Senior Year

The fall wind touches the man who hoes
His upland garden clean for spring,
While faraway autos sing
And a faraway rooster crows.

The fall wind hurries the man who goes
On foot a stony village road
In the service of his Lord,
And hugs his cassock close.

The fall wind whispers to him who knows
Only the breathless air of stacks,
Tracing in ancient books
The roots whence man arose.

The fall wind searches out all those
Who feed man's body or soul or mind;
I ask it which it will find
Me doing when next it blows.

1934

Brief Choice

Time, the imaginary stream,
In running sets a certain pace—
The long, long running downhill home—
That will not let us stay in place
Nor turn back upstream toward the spring

Nor yet outrun it in a race,
But whether swift as at a fall
Or in green lowlands lingering
Gives us brief choice of what to bring
Unto the gathering of all.

1950

The Chance of Endless Glory

This world that was so stable,
So well beyond our sway—
We suddenly are able
To shatter it in a day;

It was the repository
For man's most dear effects,
The chance of endless glory
For mortal architects.

1950

The Letting Go

If anyone's footwork should be sure,
The organist would be the one:
Observe how punctual and pure
His notes are in a pedal run.

The slightest lingering on a key
Will show he harbors some regret
To reach for what he cannot see
For fear his balance be upset.

He has to practice prompt release,
The letting go and passing on;
Note after note must speak and cease
The instant its occasion's gone.

1934

16

Our Several Houses

Notice to Passengers

A poem was the first chariot,
And the first passengers either thought
They were in the hands of a fool, or not.

1951

Dark Journey

Bleak evening overtakes the town:
Some lamps are lit, some shades are down
To keep the universal gloom
Out of the personal living room.

I, meanwhile, traveling north by night,
Steering behind my lonely light,
Must traverse thoroughfare and street
Till I regain my square of heat.

1950

Dark Theater

Soon as our two stores close at eight
The twisted street at once looks late—
A hollow stage-set coldly lit
Whose play has failed, whose cast has quit.

The man on foot who has the nerve
To enter round the snow-banked curve
Under the dead opposing fronts
Acts hunted, or as one who hunts.

1951

Coming Home

Our several houses sit so still
And separate in snow
As if in hopes to take no chill
By keeping dimly huddled so,

That one might long, as long ago,
To be coming home where college lights
And voices in rooms row on row
Collectively ignore sharp nights.

1951

Early to Bed

Early to bed
Leaves dark ahead

In which to wake
As by mistake

And hear the train
Approach and wane—

And sleep again.

1951

The Circumstances

Who came, who sent a message
The day he wrote this passage?
What was his lunch, cold sausage?

Did he mind solitude,
Or was his vein so good
He hardly stopped for food?

The joy he brought to book
Does not suggest he took
Much time to talk *or* cook.

1951

Widower's Windows

Old widower saves lights
By supping early, nights,

Wipes his two dishes dry
By the last light of the sky,

Rocks some time in the dark
To settle his beans and pork,

Then feels his way to bed
Where stars attend his head.

1951

Night Windows

Night windows that you pass
On after-supper tramps
Afford you such a glimpse
Of chairbacks and pale lamps
So close beyond the glass,

That once in every street
You almost think you're meant
To see what they have to eat,
And what they burn for heat,
And how they are content.

1951

Luxury

Electric candles on the sill
Make this room radiant;
The furnace purrs under the grille.

Sit here and share what we've been sent;
Without you we can ill
Afford the luxury of content.

1950

Poor Wheeling

Likely in time of mud or slush
You'll have to steer while others push.

Though soon enough you'll have the luck
To help get someone else unstuck,

It probably won't be the party
That just lent you a hand so hearty.

But that's no reason to regret
This venturesome discharge of debt.

1951

The Yearly Whiteness

I had to shut my book
And quit my narrow room
And come and stand and look
At the apple tree in bloom;

Currents at daybreak shook
Much whiteness to its doom,
And full twelve months this took,
To please, if not me, whom?

1951

Our Pond

Seeing it dazzle through dark boles,
You might think our pond reached to the poles.

The water slapping at the wharf
Churns into something much like surf,

And I won't find the slightest fault
If you fancy the inshore breeze is salt—

Nor be surprised if some dazzled dreamer
Should wake to the hail of a London steamer.

1952

Southbound

Southbound the longest day of the year
Out of our intervales
The milk trains rumble down the rails.

The placid rivers winding near
From other pastoral fountains
Reflect red barns, white spires, green mountains.

Toward midnight miles and miles from here
At rail and power stations
Strange hands will forward these donations.

1952

Night Milking Time

Night milking time in our goat barn
With hand-hewn frame and planking worn
From daily passing, night and morn;

Across the board wall, mellowed brown,
Light from the windowed loft slants down
Through the trap door where hay is thrown;

The dusky stable facing east
Rustles with many a munching beast,
Smelling of out-of-doors, snow-fleeced.

How low in light of all the sky
The space here covered dim and dry—
And yet so generous, so high,

One tenant more would cause no cramp
If I should make a corner-camp
In here tonight—no bed, no lamp.

1951

The Egg-Hunter

One of the farmer's fondest prayers
Is, Let the pullets be good layers.

Pleasantest of his daily dangers
Is chancing upon nests in mangers.

Nothing rewards his cautious hand
Like this smooth oval contraband.

1951

The Scythe

At haying when I crop
My roadside in the sun,
Somebody's sure to stop
And show me how it's done:

"Let's see that scythe—stand back.
You want to swing her wide,
See—what *you* do is hack.
See—eas-y, let her ride."

At least the shade is cool
Where I once more, excused,
Am taught this is the tool
Men hate to see abused.

1951

Midsummer

Midsummer midday focused
In the stinging note of the locust
Advises us to make
The most of field and lake

While they are ours to take—
While the season stays on center—
Before some hint of winter
Suffuse them with an ache.

1952

Dark Under the Table

Most all of you good neighbors go to bed
As soon as it gets dark under the table,
And I would do the same if I were able—
Our daylight steps should earn our daily bread.
But there is no rest in my restless head,
And I must pass under every darkened gable,
Hearing a horse stomp deep within a stable,
Hearing a wakeful dog growl in a shed.

Under the summer moon the maples' shade
Buries our still street like a forest glade.
The emerald signal at the railway station,
Keeping us still connected with the nation,
Catches the steel of one expectant rail
That swerves to miss the moonlit mountain pale.

1952

Work for Pay

Work done for love is play.
When work is done for pay,
The first hour seems a day

As unused cords get pulled,
The mind engrosssed and dulled,
The laborer numb-skulled.

Yet though subdued to dirt
And seemingly inert,
Mind takes no lasting hurt;

Even the meanest chore
May well augment its store
Of detail and hard lore.

1950

The Church at Newark

The sermon with its gaps
Conducive to short naps
Suggests life was not planned
For us to understand.

The church, though, stovepipe-spanned,
Declares how sure a hand
Here utilized the inch
As though it were a cinch

To bend both stair and bench
Without the slightest pinch—
A plan without perhaps,
Apology, or lapse.

1951

The Academy at Brownington

In settlements established late,
The one considerable building,
Perhaps with cupola and gilding,
Is apt to be a duplicate
Of something from an earlier date.

In one hill town along my walks
The first academy, tall, gaunt,
Original as befits Vermont,
Still stands as raised of granite blocks
By its first master and his ox.

What sets originals apart
From even the most authentic fraud?
Style? No, they may be gravely flawed.
Originals are at the start
Homemade, made home for man and God.

1952

The Trouble with a Son

The trouble with a son,
You never get him done.

There's always some defect
Remaining to correct,

Always another flaw
To disappoint his pa—

Who knows how imperfection
May suffer from rejection.

1952

My Dread

I don't know where I got my dread,
But something someone long since said
At supper must have filled my head

With visions of nocturnal dealings
Where men and women without feelings
Consorted under smoky ceilings—

Not all my sunshine intercourse
With honest folk has had the force
To touch this terror at its source.

1952

The Revolt of the Hired Man

I got tired
Of being hired
To wag my tongue
At the young,

Who ought
And who ought not.
"Be better than I,"
I would sigh,

"And wiser."
Some adviser!
I quit to see
What I'd be.

1952

Schoolhouse Windowpanes

Then schoolhouse windowpanes were brave
Amid black maples and white drifts
With rosy Santas bearing gifts
We scholars would be fools to crave.

Not that resentment spoiled our fun:
Scholars are no less realistic
For being on occasion mystic.
Christmas is kind to everyone.

1951

Matinee

Flakes falling and fallen whirl
Round a woman, man, and girl
Breasting the noonday storm
A mile from any farm.

When I pull up the car
And call out, Going far?
They're glad to get inside
And gladder still to ride.

"Aggie, she had no school,
So Fred, the perfect fool,
He says never mind the blow—
Let's take her to the show."

1952

Winter Sitting

Whom wintertime confines indoors
Or to the circuit of the stores,
Post office, lunchroom, railway station,
With nothing to do but winter chores,
Become each other's occupation.

Then are the brave seen arrogant,
The patient pitifully meek,
The learned otherwise ignorant—
No sir, it is not far to seek
How any virtue makes us weak.

1951

A Game of One Old Cat

My cat grows old
And minds the cold.
No sooner out
Than he wants in—
And turnabout.
I never win.
But no great loss.
Such is the wage
We owe old age,
Which can be cross
As well as sage.

1952

Come and See

The doctor came right in with his rubbers on,
Straight through the kitchen to the downstairs bedroom.
He felt her pulse and listened to her heart,
And never spoke a word to anyone.
To her, he smiled and shook his head and sighed.
After a while he turned his chair around
And said, "Some snowfall for the time of year."
Like any workman with his rubbers on!
Still, what can we expect of anyone
But that he come and see, do what he can,
And sociably await the miracle?

1951

Spring Lambs

So tickled to be born
This genial April morn,
New lambs try out their legs
In foolish little jigs;

While I, whose time is fall,
Am startled to recall
How comical I felt
Before I heard of guilt.

1952

32

Spring's Work

Forty times empty, forty full,
Which comes to eighty for the whole
If you accept my dreamy counting,
I've passed the place, insensible,
Where if you look you see the mountain.

I'm wheeling out the winter crop
My undomestic creatures drop
Indoors, not even begging pardon,
To broadcast on the field and garden,
And I'm too tired to want to stop.

1952

Water System

With the sea inlanders keep in touch
By way each of his pasture brook—
The system seems far-fetched to such
As have a littoral outlook.

But in a system branch and trunk
Feed to a main, or thence are fed,
And even a sequestered monk
Is a member of some watershed.

1951

The Total Scene

Time whom we lump with worm and weevil
Is actually good *and* evil:
He shifts the total scene.
Excellent men and mean
And in between
Indifferently die.
Good riddance or good-by
To all.
We call this lack of bias want of taste
Because we have to call
Waste waste.

1949

Arrival

Abruptly as the shade
Of plum and alder thickets
That wintered bare as pickets
Arrives to close our glade—

Sudden as youth or maid
Claims privacy of pockets,
Immunity of lockets—
Time brings what time delayed.

1951

A Personal Terrain

At a Cello Recital

How the shore seems to the fellow
Who reaches it by cello,
How different from the seaboard
One comes to on a keyboard—

No use to ask the brain.
This personal terrain
Only the fingers touch—
And love, almost too much.

1953

A Moment in the Midst of My Time

I slipped at the corner of the barn
And put out a hand to save my balance—
And it may tax my narrative talents
To get to the upshot of this yarn:

The weathered clapboard felt so warm
I turned to look at it, amazed,
And left my hand there, either dazed
Or shaken from my dazzled norm.

What I saw was the arm of an aging fellow
In definitely seedy clothes,
Caught in a somewhat silly pose
With a barn in grey and a sun in yellow;

And there by the grace of God leaned I
A moment in the midst of my time,
A moderate man in a temperate clime,
Having once been born, having once to die.

1952

To Be Rich

Musing on what it would be to be rich,
I saw what I was looking at: the ditch
Coated with chocolate mud the thaw had left,
Of velvet texture and luxurious heft.
As if confirming a conclusion drawn,
The naked tree put golden grosbeaks on.

1954

The Twilight Tour

I
Summer domesticates the outdoors:
Of grass and gravel are the floors
Over which she pitches her tent,
Fragile and blue and impermanent;

Trees are partitions, rocks are chairs,
Roads are the hallways, and the stairs
Are hills we climb at evening, kneeling
Under the clearly holey ceiling.

II
Along the route of our evening ride
Houses and barns stand open wide
To let the out-of-doors inside.

Hay-doors reveal the half-filled mows,
White stables show, empty of cows,
Lean-to's expose harrows and plows—

Good thing for the owners we aren't thieves!
Through chamber casements under the eaves
We look right through to the backyard leaves.

III

By the ruined farm above the town
We spent the twilight looking down;
Below us in the summer heaven
The steeple clock said six, then seven.

The swallows sailed by pairs and singles
Into the barn that wanted shingles—
We estimated the expense.
I got a shock off the pasture fence.

IV

These late performers in the sky
Fight sleep, child-like, by circling high
And swooping with excited cry;

Others receive the nightly guest
With chirps of welcome soft expressed,
And nestle murmuring to rest.

V

Night, almost, in the avenue
Down which the road recedes from view;
Yet eastward out of window-holes
Framed by black boughs and massive boles,
The slopes are light where God would dwell
At evening when the world was well.

VI

After the kind of day that scorches
The wilted earth in breathless heat,
People are sitting on their porches
On both sides of the darkling street,
Just looking out between their feet.

They greet you in domestic voices
As you stroll through on your twilight tour,
And all your heart this night rejoices
That you are poor among the poor,
And share with them the temperature.

1953

39

My Native Scene

How shall I put my native scene
In spring before it puts on green?
Over the field of tousled flax
The mountain is a distant blue;
The tree that unifies the two
Is penciled in in greys and blacks.

Notice its infinite refinement
Or praise its formidable strength—
I could do either at some length.
Why not do both in the same assignment?
That's how I'll take my native view:
Good songs blend opposites, both true.

1953

The Concluding Hour

In the concluding hour
From evening chores to bed,
The sky still overcast
From the receding shower,
The right word should be said
About the day being past—
How was it, slow or fast?
What if it were our last?

Away on top of the hill
Against the leaf-dark wood
Under the soft-lit sky,
The children are on high
Repairing the old tree house
In the great maple tree—
Hark, hear them shouting still?
When back of the barn I stood
And looked just now, I could see
A white shirt, or a blouse.

40

They will come down to bed
When the warm windless hour
Fails and the day is past,
And I shall find you curled
In slumber by my side
When I come up at last
After the word is said,
And I again have tried
Conclusions with the world.

1954

The Midnight

Midsummer midnight, hot, and still
Except for the hum of motors from
The open windows of the mill.
Across the track the railway station
Is lighted too, in expectation:
The midnight mail-train, yet to come,
Stops even if they have no fare.
They'll whistle for the crossing—there.

In the comfortable semi-dark
We have been talking the time away
On a baggage cart, the agent and I,
Waiting to close the village day.
In the roaring onrush he, with a sigh,
Gets down to put on the platform light.

I wander home across the park
That waits for nothing now, to write,
While they fade southward, this goodnight.

1956

Great Sun

Great sun, source of the goodness of our sphere,
Whose setting is a heavy loss of cheer,
Your very power may cause you to appear
Capricious, as the times you burn too hot;
Your very evenness may seem unfeeling,
As when you failed us that day miles from here
In course of a wild quest for what was not—
But who accuses you of double dealing?

The little lights we of late years invent
To see by when we'd better be asleep,
What are they but excitements meant to keep
Our nights as well as daytimes discontent?
And what but your invariable dear
Disinterestedness is innocent?

1955

A Pair of Pastorals

THE BRIDAL

for Donald Ames Craig

The hottest hours of sun
Are only now begun.
The time is just eleven
But the fire is high in heaven
And will not set till seven—
Eight coming hours of heat
To thaw the hands and feet
That tingled in the clamp
Of January damp.
The making hay is sweet
With timothy and clover,
And soon it will be made—
See it begin to fade
From green to shiny grey—

42

It's time we turned it over.
Later on, if you stay,
We'll put it up in tumbles
While, maybe, thunder rumbles,
And get it under cover.

The temper of the time
Counts sitting still a crime.
But you and I don't care.
We're neither here nor there;
We're out of it, up in the air—
Not better than the rest,
Not that, but simply blessed
With this security,
Complete obscurity.
The world don't give a damn
Where you are or I am.
We're neither presidents
Nor chairmen of the board.
We're free to live by work
In the high town of Burke—
I farm some, you're a clerk.
We're free to sit on the sward
Here on this eminence
Provided by the Lord.

Though off the lanes of traffic,
We still are geographic.
Surely we have our function.
Lovers of earth, in fact,
Are acting in conjunction
Wherever they may act.
And we are far from idle.
We celebrate a bridal
Betwixt earth and the sun
Whose care has just begun
To cure the present crop
And bring the future up.

1953

43

ONE SUMMER'S DAY

Here let me spend the day,
By way of piety,
Attending to the play
Of light on the maple tree.

I seem to think I owe
Heaven or earth or both,
As honoring an oath,
The service of one slow
Summer day's silent growth.

I know if I am still
Something will seize the chance
To heal me of the ill
I took from circumstance.

And I shall see this much
In quietness: first light
Creating out of air
Color that to the sight
And gloss that to the touch
Will all the day be fair.

And I may understand,
By ten o'clock or eleven,
Why patient engineers
Such as constructed heaven
Will spend a hundred years
On one of these machines
That clothe the summer land
In their perennial greens.

Nothing I want to do
At noon or one or two
But enter this green peace
Under a life-time lease
As off-and-on co-dweller
With the run of its extents
From attic to root-cellar,

Letting past and future fade
And the whole world condense
To a green thought in green shade:
To pay attention to
The moment and the tree
Is surely to renew
Our life eternally;
This is my notion of
Eternal life and love.

Nothing we need to know
Between now and the night
But how a man may grow,
By solitude and yearning,
To apprehend a fact.
This is the only learning,
This is sufficient act.
I have my life to write.

1958

Dark Portal

At my first approach to a covered bridge
As a child
When going to ride
Was a privilege,
The dark portal looked so small
Through the windshield of the truck—
It made me duck.
We must be too wide
And much too tall.

My father smiled.
"Don't worry, we'll fit;
We'll be the right size
When we get to the rise."
And we were, but the approach was exquisite.

1949

Outside the Gate

The child outside the iron gate,
Watching tall guests across the lawn,
Receives ideas of what goes on
That may not ever be set straight.

Such favored people must be kind,
And yet are manifestly cruel;
Absorbed they are, yet idle. Dual
Conceptions baffle a green mind.

A child outside an iron gate,
Watching tall guests across a lawn,
Will form ideas of what goes on—
Will just be lucky not to hate.

1950

Of Live Possessions

(Hayford's Law)

Children and pets, please note:
When one is pleased to dote,
Your part is to be grateful;
When you presume to expect
Indulgence, you seem hateful
And may be sharply checked.

That any live possession
May thus commit aggression
Does seem unfortunate,
But in a closed universe
Love is the source of hate,
And favor is a curse.

See that you stand in awe
From childhood of this law,
To ward off desperation
And heal the cruel cut
Whenever god or nation
Moodily says tut tut.

1954

Whom Contradictions Ravage

I
Whom contradictions ravage,
Enacting gentlemen
Though actually savage—
Most live to fight again.

II
Some give in to despair
Seeing they're sure to lose,
Caught in a man's affair
With boys' equipment—shoes
Sixes instead of twelves—
Some kill themselves.

III
Who in our circle are serene
Excepting those whom innocence,
Despite the usual guilt, keeps clean,
Faithful, and full of confidence?
Though sensing the impermanence
Not of flowers only and fine weather
But of men's civil life together,
They take no blame for the disaster
They may or may not help bring on faster.
Yes, those we know that are serene
Are surely those whom innocence,
Despite some guilt, keeps clean.

1954

Address to Those Who Don't Go to Meetings

Address the college—
I, dressed formal?

First, I'm no scholar—
I'm short on knowledge—
I lack for a text.
And next,
I've mislaid my collar,
Which never felt normal.

Can't I in these clothes
Address me to those
Who don't go to meetings?

Greetings,
Lone farmers and fishers
And unemployed wishers
Who don't join the crowd
Because you're too proud
Of not being rich,
Or else haven't a stitch
And so aren't allowed;
You authorized hermits
And you without permits
Who'd hate to be named—

You think I've been tamed.
Oh no, there you're wrong.
I just half belong
To the social order.
I don't and I do.
I live on the border.
Ask them if they trust me—
You'll find they've discussed me—
They class me with you.

I join them from love—
Of lots of their ways—
And there's a bad phrase
To be guilty of.

Let me lay this before you:
You've a right to be wild.
So let them ignore you
And don't feel exiled.

1953

The Resident Worm

for Donald Ames Craig

The pitcher plant makes a living by
Enticing living things to die
In quest of ruinous delight.
It keeps an adjutant that thrives
On this rich harvest of lost lives—
A resident worm or parasite.

On the other hand, the goldenrod
Survives invasion by a worm
That dines upon its endoderm
And winters in a private pod—
An ugly but benignant cyst
That isolates the colonist.

So life is given and taken in ways
That are too hard for us to praise—
Inhuman is the word for God.

1955

To the Birds

They sent me to the birds
To see life without words.
The birds, they said, have song;
They do not sit and talk
All day of right and wrong—
They fly and sing daylong.

All right, I took a walk.
Returned, I ask, Which birds?

The beneficial hawk
Whose eye and scissor beak
Eliminate the weak
And keep the small breeds strong?

The amiable wren
That is such friends with men
Though under the suspicion
Of looting others' nests
To cut down competition
For local grubs and pests?

The catbird that's so smart
It makes up its own song
Fresh as it goes along—
Except, of course, the part
That mocks the inborn verses
Some standard bird rehearses?

The cowbird that reneges
When it comes to hatching eggs—
The archetypal hood,
Planting its little yeggs
In someone else's brood?

It's well to be on the wing
And very well to sing,
But I'm still questioning
The ethics of the thing.

1953

Of Woods and Waves

What the land would be if it could is forest:
Forest it was until men cleared it;
To forest it reverts when farms decay.
Earth's virtue must express itself in trees.

Water's comes out in restless waves and tides
Which, chafing at their million shores
By day and night as they have done forever,
Would also overrun the land if able.

In us, children of woods and, earlier, waves,
The pulsing of deeps long restrained,
The airy urge of high luxuriance.
The trees have better opportunities.

1956

Handmade

Poems are still made by hand
So slow is the demand—
All somewhat different,
Each an experiment
In actual delight.
Not many turn out right;
Few households have a sound
Fresh specimen around.

1955

The Principle Is Growth

Of moving immobility
The model is a tree.
Compliance, fixity,
The tree has both.
The principle is growth.
The essence is to live,
To stay put and yet give,
To sway and still not snap—
And what it takes is blood or sap.

1954

The Poor

We see them keeping warm
Before and after storm
As prisoners to whom
The world assigns one room,
Its door and window cracks
Stoppered with burlap sacks—

We see them meanly holed
Up, rags all helter-skelter
In shells that aren't much shelter
At twenty-five below
Against the cleanly cold,
The glittering stars and snow.

1954

Our Managers

In offices a long way off
Where even now lights will be burning,
Our managers with the nervous cough
Keep the old state machinery turning
That should deter some other nation
In justice' name and for God's sake
From taking what we might well take
In God's name and for justice' sake
If we were in their situation.

1956

Law

Fear is the fatal feeling
That comes from seeing Law
Order its iron dealing:

Nobody ever saw
Nature or county court

Without inquiring why
Mercy is in such short
Supply.

1955

The House That I Jacked

The builder of this house,
Long dead, who still plays host
To me and my cat and her mouse,
Was so adroit a man
I grieve to vex his ghost
By cluttering his plan.
He set a single post
Where it was needed most;
I liked his wide clean span
Of solid cellar timber.
But age had made it limber;
A sag came in the floor.
I had to prop and shore.
It irks me to bequeath
My heirs an underneath
Legged like a centipede
Instead of a trim steed.

1953

Original

Seems our original sinner
Was also our beginner—
Origin of our life.

He promptly blamed his wife,
Who turned to blame the snake,
Which graciously stood mute.

Thus the original man
Impatiently began
To have and eat his cake—

Or in this case his fruit.

1955

Electric Night

That desert element the dark
Our predecessors felt so frightful
Takes on the comforts of a park
With lights, noise, company delightful.

Midnight is not the void it was
When people slept from eight till four;
December, once black winter's core,
Twinkles with parties and applause.

My, how we tame the elements—
Silence and darkness, cold, and time—
And all for comforts whose expense
Is tedium and nervous crime.

1950

Snow in the Trees

Snow is a sleepy motion in the trees
That takes the eye with business ever witty.
And I suppose it's snowing in the city
Amongst the sheer rectangularities
Of light-shot business and apartment blocks
In avenues distinguished for their glitter.
Oh, I am neither envious nor bitter;
The city's fine, I would not change my walks.

I might be tempted to betake me there
If city folk were minded to produce
Elegance of equal or superior use
To, say, a Wren facade or a Mozart air.
It must be I still have the old-style notion
Our works should fill the air with cheerful motion.

1953

Christ Coming

Christ coming through split cloud
Unto his mother's womb
At the turning of the year
May not have seen the crowd
That took up every room
As anything to fear.

Later, leaving, lonely,
Suffering at their hand
By act of the elect,
He may have asked why only
The unsuspecting stand
Unanimously suspect.

1954

Tame Toms

Your nose against the window bright
From snowbanks under the street light,
In the dead living-room you crouch
Along the back-rest of the couch,
Watching the passing of the night

Who tries to draw us out to her
By making the bare branches stir
As if to taunt us who prefer,
Both you and I, to watch her pass,
Dozing by turns within thin glass.

1952

Compact Speech

Spare land and lean,
So briefly green
And so long white
In northern night,
You teach
In compact speech
The economy I mean:

Life on hard ground
Keeps people sound,
Love of bare trees
Tells what we do—
We who
Inhabit you—
For luxuries.

1956

Not Much of a Career

Not much of a career
The man may say of me
Who's risen year by year
To some good presidency.

But I say let a man
Ask nothing in advance
Nor bother with a plan,
But take his gains from chance.

What bargains we see made
In most man-made careers
Where all we have to trade
Is all we have—our years.

1956

Processional with Wheelbarrow

Our Place

Our place is ringed with fatal deeps
Where to falter is to fail for keeps.

Yet if we'd never left dry ground
We wouldn't know the world is round;

If we'd never set foot on the sky
We wouldn't know that we can fly;

Nor would we know if we didn't die
Whether we living signify.

1958

In My Great Content

In memory of all the days I've hated,
The featureless and lost, unnamed, undated
Days when I hurried through my work and waited

For some composing touch that would not come—
In memory of those, which I am from
As much as from the clear and venturesome—

I frame this tribute in my great content.
But for those days misshapen and misspent,
Should I have known what composition meant?

1957

Sonata III

Papers in piles—if I keep piling on,
What's to become of them all when I am gone?
My organ teacher must have left a shed-full—
Music that was, and most of it was dreadful.

What he did well was play and improvise—
Which won him a life-long name for being wise;
Like most men who aspire to paper fame
He should have trusted a lot more to flame.

One paper from his pile came down to me—
The manuscript of Organ Sonata III
Inscribed in German to some mutual friends
Who moved away and left it on my hands.

Poor old Sonata III—I can't return you;
Does simple piety say keep or burn you?

1960

Sky Pond

Far more susceptible are you, fair water,
Level and limpid, than the coarse dry land—
The sky's reflective and
Most filial daughter.

I should have lived where you are never frozen
And summer does not cost a winter's price,
Had not my fathers chosen
Seven months of ice.

1957

The Mirror of My Realm

In the corner back beyond,
Where the brook enters the spruces,
I have a little pond;
Its banks are smoothly lawned
And it has several uses.

The cattle come to drink,
A frog lives in the brink,
It is my swimming pool;
I take there what I think
Is the only sport that's cool.

On the cool grass I sit
At dusk and look at it,
Composing clouds and the elm
That rises opposite—
The mirror of my realm.

It takes far things and tall
And lays them at my feet
While sleepy thrushes call.
I haven't to leave my seat
To have my world complete.

1953

Latter Days

Persuaded that it will be lonely later
When the lights are all out and the people gone,
I who am always an impatient waiter
Say, almost, Let the loneliness come on:
Let winter wind imprison me inside
Where no fire warms the rattling passages,
My future poor in hope, my past in pride,
With no one present but the Presences;

And let us try what loneliness entire
Will do to a mind that sometimes chose itself
Instead of company around a fire,
Or found its company along a shelf—
Let's see if I shall have the wit to bless,
Like early ills, this latter loneliness.

1953

Abroad at the Winter Solstice: A March

With bough and with berry
Behold men make merry
At news of the blessing—

The human made holy
And held to be slowly
In good will increasing.

By hedgerow and fireside
In good time and dire tide
All dimly progressing,

By starlight and candle
The pastoral sandal
Beats on without ceasing.

1949

Sweet Death

O come sweet death, sang Bach,
Not instancing his own,
The man from Eisenach
Who kept the night alone,

Busy as it grew late
To wake the patient morn
With his own intricate
Simplicities for horn.

1950

Overseer of the Poor

The poor men's God that gives them sleep
Is not proved stingy just because
You may regard the gift as cheap.

Let them sleep sweetly on their straws
While rich men count expensive sheep.
God of the rich there never was.

1955

Goats in Pasture

Their bony heads untaxed by need of moving,
Changing, repairing, laying by,
Goats keep a comprehensive eye
On the condition of the sky—
Such store they set on keeping dry—
And live attentively, without improving.

1949

The Courthouse at Manchester

The courthouse front, both square and slender,
Is thus of that ambiguous gender
Wherein our fathers used to render
Their minds' austerity and splendor.

Within, republican yet regal,
The room surmounted by the eagle
Has seldom heard a plea inveigle
Their justice to be less than legal.

In honor to our sires who slumber,
Let us grow fit to join their number,
Who left sound forms and noble lumber
To liberate us, and encumber.

1947

The House at Waterford

Some who admire your adamantine twelve-by-twelves
And your low-ceilinged square apartments and broad hallways
Are in no case to live so sturdily themselves,
Who are committed to quick gains and not to always.

Some who admire the mountains from your dirty attic
And would restore you for your own sake and the view
Are looking for large leisure lost, aristocratic,
Which they imagine they could have by having you.

1958

Interior

Stairs climb and closets hide,
Chambers communicate,
Hallways run back inside
Past open doors that wait;

Portraits peer over chairs,
Books cover what they know—
The wonder is one dares
To sit surrounded so.

1951

On the Opening of a Superhighway

They are almost all gone who can recall
How any range of hills was once a wall,
And a hollow was a room and not a hall.

A change was a half-day's walk to the opposite range;
A wonder was a visit to the Grange
In the next hollow—strange street, new and strange.

A treat was local talent playing parts,
Dressed up and mannered so to steal our hearts,
Which seldom had the comfort of the arts.

And from these separate rooms a few went forth,
On bands of gravel winding south and north—
The few that glorified their place of birth.

1957

The Autumn Voice

Time was, the summer guest
Took with him faring west
The heart out of my breast,

Within whose aching hollow
Autumn cried Follow, follow
Summer and sun and swallow

To streets where brick and stone
Bask in the genial zone,
And no child cries alone.

1952

Social Interlude

The busyness of stores
Attracts me to their doors
To hear what's going on,
Or what has gone.

So I am told who's dead,
Expectant, sick abed;
What boys are hard to handle,
What girls risk scandal.

Thinks I, ill is not dealt
According to the guilt,
Neither does God chastise—
Men moralize.

And hearing someone suppose
Goodness will best its foes,
I say don't give me logic—
I'll trust in magic.

1951

In the Street

Step downtown for a spool of thread
And hear the heart advise the head
On how to co-exist with dread:

The head asks how can it be thought
Men that will find a means to blot
Out half mankind will use it not?

But the heart keeps saying life's too dear;
Come in, sad reasoner: in you, here,
Is your sufficient source of cheer.

So you will find it in the street:
Scarce any heart of all you meet
Is daunted by the head's defeat.

Step downtown for a loaf of bread
Before the winter day is dead,
And you will find it as I've said.

1959

The Summer Lovers

Scuffing the mealy dryness with wet toes
Along the sunny crescent of white sand
Among the prone and splashing bathers and
The babble of small children with no woes,

The summer lovers, nearly naked, tanned,
Watching the water-skiers as they sweep
Under the blue sky over the blue deep,
Ramble an aimless hour hand in hand.

1959

The Onrush

The crow, how he flew
As the river flowed,
And the engine crew
Waved as they rode
Longside till my road
Or their rails withdrew.

And how the crow cawed
As the engine blew,
Crossing the broad
River now thawed
And boiling like brew—
Spring raised such a hue!

1960

The Beauty That Belongs to Lust

What of the beauty that belongs to lust,
Beauty that is persuaded it can trust
Itself to live where love is not discussed?

Boldness it has, and that is something surely;
What we do know of beauty, though obscurely,
Bids us pursue it for its own sake purely.

Of course we know beauty is more than body.
But guesswork on the soul is all so shoddy.
Say lust is selfish, yes, but high and gaudy.

1958

The Hound

Tell me about the hound
That after such a chase,
All gaunt and dusty, found
His master's strange new place

Way in the Western valley,
Threading at twilight, lame,
The maple-vaulted alley
In the village of no name—

Would I be so possessed?
Would something in me wild
Refuse to let me rest
Till I had found—my child?

1952

To Learn to Swim

Let the child learn to swim
Where it's too deep for him
To touch his toes to sand:
Let him right then begin
To *be* in when he's in
By doing without land.

Let him for his own sake
Require himself to make
It from the end of the dock
Out to the diving float,
Or further out, to a boat
Or some deep-water rock—

Keeping his head and breath
While buoyed by certain death.

1953

The Run-Off

We walked to the sound of water washing
Between the knolls on slopes inclined
From sun-struck snow up higher, sloshing
In rills and runnels unconfined.

We went to sleep to water wasting
Down the rock-channeled river flume,
Jarring the town with its violent hasting,
Spending in dark its delicate spume.

1958

Under All This Slate

for Robert Francis

The bulletin of the boarding school—
Seventy lads, eleven masters—
Depicts the windowed swimming pool,
Autumnal pathways edged with asters,
Stout Georgian fronts with wide pilasters.

The Headmaster is Ph.D.
(Columbia), Princeton handles French,
English has published poetry,
The Board is winnowed from the bench,
Bar, bank, and International Wrench.

Sirs, somewhere under all this slate
You lodge, I see, a lad named Feeters.
Tell us the way he bears his fate.
Not listed with your prize competers,
Is he among your hearty eaters?

1951

The Treasurer

The treasurer of the corporation
Slides daily on his sled to dinner—
As picturesque an aberration
As ever marked a man of station
As nonetheless a man and sinner.

In him this act may be the same
As drink or women in another—
It carries less expense and blame.
Whoever finds his office tame
Must show himself a man, or smother.

The treasurer, though, assumes no pose
Nor borrows gestures from the hellion
Which are but thumbing of the nose;
He stays wild-natured like the rose,
And radical in his rebellion.

1950

All He Was Sure Of

The savage standing in the wood
Had no idea of where he stood
As to some other neighborhood.

All he was sure of, standing dumb there,
Was that he certainly stood somewhere,
And when he moved on, it was from there.

Something the same with us, only worse:
Who knows, for all our prose and verse,
Where we stand in the universe?

1959

Haying: The Comfortable Words

The farmer knee-deep on the load
Shouts, Whoa you—there, it's time you whoa'd—
You haven't got to eat every minute!
Says, This has got some green stuff in it—
We've had no weather to cure such a crop—
Well, never mind, it'll be on top.
Thundering, eh? Won't get any drier.
Don't know's I want this load much higher.
Says, Shoot, I've seen it put in wetter.
Says, This is just as good as better.

1952

Processional with Wheelbarrow

With every move I've made today
Four lambs paired up to lead the way,
Or follow, in high-tailed array.

To an unheard overture
We're marching with manure
In rites that seem obscure.

What are we out to celebrate—
The Force that makes seeds germinate,
Or the Grace that makes men meditate?

From the arch look on the features
Of four of us five creatures,
I'd say the day was Nature's.

1952

74

The Furniture of Earth

The Furniture of Earth

For all its slender girth,
The elm is stout in trouble.

The butterfly's wing power
Is masked as by a flower.

The furniture of earth
Is almost rashly noble.

1950

Barn-Light

Barn-light on the blank snow
Assures me as I go
No time could be more proper:

Cattle are being fed,
No one has gone to bed—
I shall be home for supper.

1967

Early Dark

It's getting dark by four
And pitch-dark before five,
And still a fortnight more
Till the worst of it arrive
To start our yearly test
By cold and dark and sleet.
We may be at our best
When short of light and heat.

1962

The Available Day

Low in the south the distant sun
Makes his short transit of the sky
While men with outdoor work to do
Make use of the available day:

So use this shortest day of all
That when the longest night shall fall
They may head home across the white
Ready for curtained warmth and light.

1963

The Church at Midnight

The church at Christmas midnight
Let blaze through all its glass
A glorious inside;

The next night, though, the street lamp
Discoloring its cold stones
The way it always does

Was all the light there was.

1969

The Lookouts

All lighted rooms look in
On their own discipline:
Shined objects ranged about
As they have always been;

Only dark rooms look out
To watch the lights begin
Coming in other rooms,
Till soon the long street blooms.

1963

Pictures in a Geography

I
Six tin roofs clinging to an Arctic cliff
You have to climb to from a sea-borne skiff—
This may well be the end of my line if

I keep on backing to the northward from
The futuristic look of things to come—
And feeling still obliged to differ some.

II
The places people live!
The main streets that they walk,
The buildings that they see—

No picture pleases me
Like this of a business block
Remote and primitive.

III
How many a hollow hidden by a hill
Holds men and houses, hall and mill
That we have never seen and never will!

But no place is remote to them that stay there,
Nor yet to the wise that know the way there
And can return at will to spend the day there.

1961,1963,1960

An Ideal Place

The children piling off the bus
Toward dark that winter day
Did not belong to us
As parents or as teachers,
The lucky creatures.

Anonymous,
They had come home to play
From school where nobody was cross,
We seemed to think;
Out skiing by the stand of maple
Or skating on the barnyard rink
No one would try to boss.

An ideal place needs ideal people.

1962

Something Said

Nobody's out but a winter crow
And me, of course, inspector of snow.
I almost headed back, but no:

Till something occur or be made known
I'll keep my back to the valley town
Where tomorrow's already written down.

Beyond the pasture smooth as a sheet
And the grey-green spruces capped with white
Something is being said, but what?

Something about the way a rise
Articulates with trees and skies,
Which if we knew would make us wise.

1961

A Dream of Permanence

The house below the western wood
Already in blue shadow slept,
Though snow on the opposing slope
Still kept an amber radiance.

The time was only three o'clock,
Too early to be drawing in
To book and stove and curtains drawn
Against the icy tide of dark.

The place to stay was where I stood
Between the luster and the shade,
Not quite relinquishing the light,
Not quite yet yielding to the night,

But resting in the optic play
Whereby a house not even mine
Slept in a dream of permanence
Between an ebbing and a flood.

1958

Winter Company

Inviting you to tea
That bitter winter day
I hoped you'd comfort me
By hearing what I had to say.

But no, full of your own concerns
You came, and what to do;
Not even taking turns,
You let me comfort you.

1975

Out in the Dark of the Year

I notice as I walk
Out in the dark of the year
Windows square with light,
And wonder if the talk
Within is also clear
And confidently bright
And comfortable with cheer.

And what should fortunate folk
Conclude as snug they sit
After the winter's day,
Between slow puffs of smoke
Enjoying wine and wit?
I like to think that they
Grow wise by what they say.

1954

In Wilderness

Standing alone in wilderness
Among some low snow-bearing firs,
I called to mind my ancestors
Who knew enchantment or distress
In solitude where nothing stirs.

Snow-colored sky, snow-covered ground
Tufted with fixed and silent trees—
How many of my fathers found
Their fortitude enhanced by these,
How many sighed for stir and sound?

Me, I'm divided in my mind:
Patience I shall not always lack
To leave the settlements behind
And keep the solitary track—
But now, time I was getting back.

1958

For Mr. Bentley

*Wilson A. Bentley, 1865-1931,
of Jericho, Vermont, took
photomicrographs of thousands
of snowflakes.*

Ever since you concluded
No two snowflakes the same,
Production men have brooded
On the production game:

Think how long it would take
To research each design;
It's that, or give each flake*
The freedom to combine,

Just not repeating once,
Infinite variants
(Hexagonally based)
According to its taste—

The highest elegance
Producing the least waste.

*18,000,000 per cubic foot

1968

The Sun Stays Busy

The sun stays busy melting the snow,
The soil drinking the flood,
The river handling the overflow,
The wind drying the mud—

The whole machinery functioning
To turn our winter into spring.

1974

Unpainted Farm

Bare tree, dull ground, unpainted farm
Compose a scene of sober charm
That does the looker-on no harm;

But let spring start to generate
Green grass, green leaves—see spring create
Temptations to luxuriate.

1962

Ring Dance

Earth in her springtime heat
Discarding the cool sheet
In which she slept so sound,
Dance in a ring around,
Children, with your bare feet
Treading her tawny ground,
And take some happiness
Before she starts to dress
And give you such good haying
You have no time for playing.

1966

May Morning

Aloft, my neighbor mends his roof;
Below but not far, not aloof,
I get my garden ready for seed.
He talks to himself about showers and speed,
I pay my respects to witchgrass and weed.

Thoreau had confidence in Nature's
Magnanimous wisdom for all her creatures.
Hard seeing how this applies to man,
Where trouble seems to be part of the plan—
Some days I *can't* see it, blamed if I can.

But—shine on his roof and keep him calm,
And let me manage one tranquil psalm.

1952

Spring Prom

In halls where no one's studying,
In cars convertible and sports,
The campus swarms with couples in shorts
Who celebrate the rites of spring
With lubricants in cans and quarts.

Dry year on the academic heights
Whose moistening takes two days and nights . . .
But then I've always been non-plused
To figure how these numbing rites
Are thought to serve either love or lust.

1961

In Case of Rain

I wouldn't order a parade
Which counts on sunshine for success
For fear I might feel overpaid
For righteousness
If the sun obeyed—
Or worse, betrayed
In case of rain.

What would I stand to gain
By being made
To love a day the less
For coming in a liquid dress?

1963

First Day of Summer

So hushed the pupils at their play
You'd never guess this is the day
When school lets out for the whole summer.

Across the common, even dumber,
Vacationing city folk in pairs
Face newspapers in rocking chairs.

Maybe it's not for me to say—
I am a relative newcomer—
But someone ought to say hurray.

1953

Roses Ahead

No roses yet?

        No roses yet.

Why not?

        It's been too cold and wet.

Not right for roses.

        No, don't fret.

Summer *is* young . . .

        Young as she'll get.
Roses ahead, and you regret
It isn't time for roses yet!

1964

Cloud at Evening

Piled into creamy wall and tower
Or leveled into field and park
Where time stands always at the hour
Before dusk yields to dark,

The great cloud, reddening, sails for Spain.
This was my vision as a youth
Of Heaven, citadel and plain,
And I half think it was the truth.

1957

Wanderer's Choice

What is to fix the wanderer's choice
In countryside where every farm
Combines the wild and civil charm
That makes the wanderer's heart rejoice—
Which road will have the winning voice?

Rejoice, and in the same breath mourn:
For each farm derelict and lorn,
For every family displaced,
A little world has been erased
Whose like will not again be born.

1958

The Summer Hotel at Jefferson

My grandfather in his White Mountain hotel
Had little but room and board and the view to sell
To people who wanted just room and board and a view
And came on the train for the summer with nothing to do

But hike and climb, picnic and take the sun,
And ride the carriage road up Washington—
For them the keeper of a summer hotel
Had to have little more than peace to sell.

1960

The Slide

That day the mountainside let go
To bury everything below

The folks at one farm in its path
Ran both sides from the arriving wrath.

The slide, dividing, spared the place,
But buried them without a trace.

When hell breaks loose the place to hide
Is either in- or not in- side.

1966

Up on the Hill

I have been up on the side of the hill
And looked at the world till I looked my fill.

I walked and watched two distant showers,
Then sat and dreamed the hill was ours.

How does it feel to be on high?
Full as you hope to feel when you die.

1970

High on a Warm Hill

High on a warm hill
With an evening view
Over what would have been a duchy or two,

And everything still
But a whippoorwill
In the dark wood over the road,

A couple grown white
Are talking away
On the porch with the front yard unmowed—

What about? Who can say?
But maybe their day—
Their time, as viewed from their height.

1963

The Exception

One sharp old man we knew
Died doing what he loved to do,

Addressing our town meeting.
Some talked as though this might be cheating:

He should have died confined,
Out of our sight, out of his mind.

Sadly it must be said
Few men drop elegantly dead.

1963

Calm Time

Calm time tonight: no water coming ashore;
No traffic on the pond, not even an oar
To dim the image of our dominant mount
That tapers upside-downward to a point
And floats in a woody frame on the watery floor.

1966

Mountain Churchyard

How in its headlong rush
Down to the distant river
Black water on black rocks
In overhanging brush
Forever spends itself
Upraising the white hush
In which they live forever.

1965

Her Burial

Out on the hill she lies now, nights,
Who lately lived with us indoors
Under much lesser lights
Than this full moon and stars,

And in the daytime, sun,
Unstopped by any barrier
But one:
The ton of earth on top of her.

1965

91

The Picture of God

While God was plainly King of Spain
His powers and privileges were plain:
He reigned, and He could make it rain.

When kings sat down to hold disputes,
Like business men, in business suits,
He faded—cape, sword, riding boots.

1966

Our Beginnings

Born with a fault you'd think
Might drive a man to drink,
I took instead to ink,
Writing, Look friends,
How our beginnings haunt our ends!

Too open to attack,
Too slow in hitting back—
This is the sort of lack
That nothing mends,
And whose beginning haunts our ends.

I had to learn to be
One who raged silently.
Don't bother telling me
How one pretends
That no beginnings haunt *his* ends.

1958

The One at Midnight

I just started late—
I just missed the one:
When the clock got to eight
I was only at seven,
Though I thought I was even.

I didn't start counting
Till the clock had begun.

I got to eleven,
My loss never mounting
Above minus one.
I stopped at eleven,
Forever undone.

1966

Fieldstone Wall

The stone with too few faces
May fit just one of the places.
Misplaced, it may well fall.
But the builder of the wall
Isn't meant to hunt all day
For where it's meant to lay.
And yet, to stay well paid
He'll see each stone well laid.
Good placements, even ideal,
Keep making stone walls real.

1972

One Thing You Learn

One thing you learn is, most joints leak,
In pipes and porch-roofs, pockets, pens,
And people's mouths, women's and men's,
That have been trusted not to speak.

Or take a car as a case in point:
My car, perhaps a case unique,
Leaks something else from every joint.
The perfect union is yet to seek.

1957

Possession of a Gun

This giving anyone
Possession of a gun
Is good of us, of course;

But what's to hinder need
From shading into greed
For such a good as force?

1965

Superfluous Sweetness

Searching the town you travel through
For signs of what the people do
To give their local lives completeness,
See touches of superfluous sweetness
Round eaves and doorways in the wood,
Put there to show the neighborhood
A worldly way of being good.

1970

Showplace

A noble house, I told my host;
What do you like about it most—
The paneling, the wide facade,
The panorama from the yard?

But he said, Oh, I like it all:
I stand entranced in the front hall—
But what if, having such a place,
I fail to show it in my face?

1964

The Stone Front

Floodlights illuminate the faults
Of the unfortunate church front
Which has the air of having been drawn
By the rector's geometric child
As a doodle during history class.

Hard for a child to refrain from filling
Big empty triangles and squares
With smaller triangles or circles;
Hard for adults to resist displaying
The only stone facade in town.

1969

Evensong

As dusk obliterates
The sober stones and slates
That keep the church substantial,

Ripe red and purple plays
The glass in the chancel bays—
To streets outside the chancel.

1967

The Lean-To

The lean-to like a vine
Half hides the sweet sharp line
Of the classic brick old-timer—
But then, no line less fine
Could half afford a climber.

1966

Thistles

Oh, thistles in the field
Grow three feet tall and yield
Great thorny tubular blooms
Crowned high with purple plumes.

But these that grow in the yard
Find the going rather hard:

Thwarted by weekly mowing
To one flat leaf-set showing,
They live by playing possum—
Live without hope of blossom.

1962

Under the Barn

Under the barn I crept
Where only dark is kept
To see what posts forgotten
Were fallen or grown rotten.

By my extension light
I crossed a sort of height
And wriggled down a hill,
And, lo, the sagging sill

Without a post to its name.
Well, none but me to blame
For being slow to treat
With the dark beneath my feet.

1951

Transactions

Rhubarb leafstalks
Cupped at the base
Catch drops of dew
To grow tall on
And feed us.

Goldfinches gather
Milkweed down
To line the nest
Where soon they'll feed
Their young.

Thimbles of dew,
Beakfuls of down—
On such transactions
Thrives a nice
Economy.

1963

Barn Swallow

Your barn swallow is a born barnstormer,
A daredevil of a performer:
See him mount almost out of sight
And, taking passage on a draft,
Slip forward, sideways, even aft;
Then skim the grass but never light,
And once more climb—
He must be having a high time—
I would, if I had his air craft.

1963

Sauntering South

for Howard Frank Mosher

Sauntering south in sight
Of long blue mountains on the right,
We naturally spoke at length of letters
And the ambition of our betters—
Twain, Hawthorne, Melville, Dickinson—
To represent the many and the one,
And how their formulas
Have helped us say what is, or was,
The status of two persons of good will
Afoot at dusk on a summer hill.

1971

Summer School

Evening revives the summer school:
After the hot day's drowsy classes
How pleasantly the hour passes
With changing into something cool
And strolling over level grasses

To dinner and the evening reading.
The visiting poet has the breeding
Not to bring up the lone despair
In winter on the city square
That gave him such things to declare.

1962

Poor Oxford

Poor Oxford in disgrace
With fortune and men's eyes
For failing in your plays
And sonnets to disguise

Your Queen's known mind and body,
You hid your wounded name
To frustrate future study
And signed away your fame—

Vacating your estate
To make a phantom great.

1972

Wood Thrush

The thrush within the wood
Retired
Is so designed
For singing to his mate

He has it understood
He can't be hired
To fete
Publics of any kind—

So privately admired
For being good
He doesn't mind
Not being great.

1966

Lovely Use

Love makes such lovely use
Of sensuality
That otherwise runs loose,

Or else is *not* expressed
But left to atrophy
As when old men choose rest—

I here and now engage
To prove that love is the
One remedy for age.

1964

Lovers at Leisure

for Arthur and Nancy Cloutier

As lovers at leisure day and night
Who see no end to our delight

Let's love each other and everyone
As though the world were just begun

And the only way to run it right,
As lovers at leisure day and night.

1960

Luck to Lovers

Let lovers all be lucky
Under the Sunday sun,
Both tongue-tied or both talky—
Their inclinations one:

To give themselves a cooling
Splash at a waterfall,
Or sun themselves while fooling
On new grass soft and small . . .

Feed them on lovers' food:
That's mutual desiring
And simultaneous mood—
And the same rate of tiring.

1966

The Bed

Back there where we were staying,
There waiting was our bed
When we had visited
A palace or a tomb
And wanted to resume
Our interrupted playing:

There we could hardly wait
To stretch out face to face
In our own time and place
After these monuments
To stolen opulence—
Most history is hate.

1972

Capital of a Small Kingdom

The cloisters are a gem,
And by a native master,
But right next door to them
The Royal Choir School
Amounts to a disaster,
And by a native fool.

Oh for a city once
With nothing in it but
Really distinguished fronts—
And not too many of them,
So that a patriot
Could altogether love them.

1973

Balance

Paired windows on both sides of a door
Once held the balance we looked for.

In music the same thing was true:
The theme returned, half old, half new;

And the counter-theme in the theme's embrace
Was what held everything in place.

1952

Inside Meets Outside

In cottage or in college hall
Inside meets outside at the wall,

Beyond which, no more terminal
However far we fly or fall.

1966

Numbers

We measure poems in feet
And music by the beat
To get the exact amounts
That make them just complete.
In any trade that counts
There is a life well spent
Where meaning is measurement.

1965

Of Keyboard Runs and Trills

All I can show for skills
Is just enough command
Of keyboard runs and trills

To whet my appetite:
I try to understand
Great flying by small flight.

1966

Working Model

Though any hull's a thin
Shell easy to crush or rip,
To the sailor in the ship
The beautiful word is *in*.

Your smart ship model, though,
Solid from keel to rail,
Was never meant to sail,
Was only meant for show.

My model, carved with a knife,
Hollowed, and tightly decked,
Worked, and though less correct
Had room inside for life.

1962

Prologue to a Poem

Here is a formulation
Of local oddity
To stand for all Creation
Tersely and handily—
And in its own right be
A lower-case creation.

1963

To Sum Up

Well may the aging poet yearn
To sum up all he's lived to learn
In a large work classical and great.

He may do better, though, to turn
Back to his small songs sharp and straight,
Loving what he loved early, late.

1950

Sweat

If it shows signs of sweat
It isn't finished yet.

Sweat over it until
Your art conceals your skill.

Effort succeeds; success
Is looking effortless.

1968

My Frame

The more my frame decays
The more I ply the art
Of fitting phrase to phrase

And framing them in rhyme
So they won't fall apart
With me, but last some time.

1968

My Notes

My presence in the house
Will be notes everywhere
Urging you and your spouse
And children to beware
The only door, which sticks,
And which if you don't fix
Will fix you, out or in,
Depending where you've been.

1971

Funnyman

I never dared be funny as I could
For fear I'd do more harm than good.

If I should be as funny as I can
I might half split some risible man.

Too bad I couldn't document this thesis,
But I couldn't risk your going to pieces.

1970

Two Birds

(With One Stone)

I
No wonder *grackle*'s a sad word—
The grackle's a sad bird:

He hasn't any song, he squawks;
He has no hop, he flatly walks.

Ill-tempered too, he drives away
Nice birds who'd like to stay.

Unfortunate his whole design—
Nothing about him you'd call fine.

How burdensome to be a bird
For whom nobody has a good word!

II
At the opposite pole
Is the oriole

Of golden throat
And golden note

And golden name.
Is he to blame

For taking what
No grackle's got?

Why, that's your duty
If born a beauty.

1963

107

Awful Origins

Jumbled against the sky,
Our mountains testify
To awful origins.
Their history begins
With fire that heaved them high
In the twinkling of an eye,
Then ice that ground them down
While centuries looked on.

1963

On Going

He keeps on going because he wants to go—
How can you see what's there if you stand still?

Oh, he stops on the bridge to hear the river flow,
He stops to admire the view from every hill;

But he has no plans for getting anywhere,
And where night overtakes him he doesn't care.

1961

108

At Large on the Land

First Light

At first light in the sky
Songbirds on every perch
Already are awake
Singing as if in church
To celebrate daybreak—

Till light enough to fly.
Once they can see to search
For breakfast, it's good-by.
Strangely, this quiet wood
Is where that choir stood.

1979

The Wash

Already on the line
Sunning and well astir,
The wash'll be dry by nine
Or earlier.

The catbird in the bush
Is helping things along;
He gives the air a push
With his mad song.

1966

Wild Raspberries

Gathering raspberries
In early morning cool
In the shadow of the house,

I gain a wild dessert
Given to birds and me—
And guarded by such thorns.

1982

Memphremagog

Blue morning lake with no work to do
But carry a boating tourist or two
Around that far peninsula
And so off into Canada,
Or yield an amateur a fish,
I cannot help but wish
Your shipping were still someone's living:
Sport seems a short thing to be giving.

1964

Ring of Hills

On this high hidden farm
Are we so far from harm—
Will any ring of hills
Wall out the worldly ills?

The ring has double force:
Keeps out some ills, of course,
But any that begin
Here it keeps in.

1966

112

A Place

No matter how we happened here—
What matters is to keep our cheer:
A place is only somewhere to be;
It only reaches as far as you see.

This place, where life has all but ceased,
Gives on an early, open east;
Even a valley known as blest
May be obstructed in the west.

Out of a stale and swampy south
The shower may come to break a drouth,
And the ragged notch in the mountains north
Stands ready to serve our going forth.

1936

Blackberrying on Equinox

Three hours from now that train
Down in the dust of noon
Will skirt the Champlain shore
Where you boys will be swimming.

See you tomorrow, son,
If we pick berries enough,
And sell them to the store,
To pay the round-trip fare.

1966

What It Took to Win

As a boy I never won a single fight.
I started some when shoved or called a sissy,
And tried to finish plenty when hit first.
I wasn't afraid of hitting or getting hit,
But never quite had what it took to win.
"Say uncle!" "Uncle," I'd say, and homeward march,
Mad all over at the rotten system
And the unbeatable, by me, world.

1964

Wrong Design?

If man was meant as a success,
Was something wrong with the design?

A head for drawing up divine
Machinery's no good unless

The heart is also very fine.

1957

The Committee to Revise the Universe

Yes, yes, the universe,
So various and vast
And visually pretty—
The trick is partly floral—
I move the universe
Be charged by this committee
With being in the last
Analysis immoral.

You call that system Law
Where most preserve their pelts
By skinning someone else?
Is anyone in awe
Of Rule that leaves the upright
Prey to the parasite?
Is any town run worse!
Most places it's agreed
Goodness is to succeed
And evil be undone,
At least in the long run.

All those in favor? Passed.
Let's draft some bills:
I move worms live on pills . . .

1957

What Is

I'm always doubtful whether
What is will hold together.

I call it pure dumb luck
When nothing comes unstuck.

How did I get so sure
The present won't endure?

I got it from the past:
What was is what didn't last.

1957

Some Failures

Some failures are so absolute
They're almost cute:
The signboard with the words too small,
The ballplayer who's afraid of the ball,
The news-announcer who can't read,
The automobile with more speed
Than the highways can accommodate,
The modern sovereign state
That's so much worse than a castle
It can't keep out a foreign missile—
Failure this absolute
Is almost cute.

1953

The Tractor

Printing a dented track
Over the rolling meadow
As it putts forth and back
In the little leaves' light shadow—

Free as toy wheels print roads
In the dirt by the kitchen door—
It rambles with many loads
At large on the land once more.

1960

Spring Tide

Of signs that spring is come,
One, less remarked than some,
Is the multiple dull drum

Of sap in empty pails.
Noons when the sun prevails
Over late March's gales,

Along the streaming roads
In mountain neighborhoods
You come on sugar woods

Knee-deep in blazing snow
Where pails drum high, drum low,
With this sweet tidal flow.

1952

The Blossoming Tree

Amid the lemon-greenery
Wherewith the woodland is alight,
Amid this lacy scenery
Is here and there a blossoming tree
All spicily englobed in white—
'Mid leafage no less gossamer,
The petals of a blossomer.

1952

Summer-People

Our earliest summer-people, birds
In hungry flocks blue, black, and brown
Blow into town
From wintering afar.
Enthusiastic guests,
They take us as we are
And help themselves to thirds
Of worms-in-clover,
And stop to look us over
Or stay to build their nests,
Wasting no words
In asking our consent
Or what's the rent—
And then return such thanks
From greening boughs and banks.

1953

Still Here

With our great backyard burst
Of cherry bloom by day
And hyla chime by night

We've come through winter's worst,
And still are here to say
Thank God we're still all right

And ready for the first
Of May.

1970

Mail-Time in May

Well before mail-time, on the grocery stoop
He settles, favoring one legless stub,
First of the winter-death-diminished group
Who hold their middle-of-the-morning club
Outdoors in Maytime at the village hub.

Unmoved he sights along his fireless pipe
At local politics and passing fashion
A fearless eye and a mind robustly ripe
From former partisan participation—
Superior now to scorn, and to compassion.

1952

The Things I Teach

Some nights I wake and wonder whether
The things I teach are worth the bother:

The things I know that can't be taught,
Or even said, or rightly thought—

Such as the way a keyboard phrase
Is felt to ripple as it plays,

The way our tight sonata form
Can even accommodate a storm—

Some nights I lie and wonder why
Teach, what I can teach is so dry.

1962

Teachers' Pay

As I walked out to smell the May,
In a darkened window on my way
A child was singing herself to sleep
With the song I taught her grade today.
Oh, teachers get nice things to keep,
To supplement their teachers' pay.

1962

View of the Village

Our houses, white on the whole,
Stand deep in a salad bowl;
You see their peaked gables
Peering through oval maples.
More fields than you can count
Pile toward the somber mount.

1951

High Town

Some towns of ours are so up in the air
You wonder how they hang on up there.
You almost expect the street to lurch
From your added weight on its tilted perch;
But no, it's on granite, a store and church
And six houses well out of the valleys of change—
They look across mountains, range beyond range.

1951

Checkerboard

Here where green hills are dark
With forest, bright with field
Which rows of maples mark
In quarters like a shield—

Here where this checkerboard
Is capped with cumulus,
A stay-at-home is lord
Of scenes luxurious.

1951

The Blaze of Summer

Amid the blaze of summer
Under the high sun
I have to count the number
Of days this has to run:

More coming than gone by.
Good. This should dull that drumming
On how my main supply
Reads more gone by than coming.

1972

Shower on the House

It knocks on the roof with liquid knuckles,
Envelops the porch in gutteral chuckles,
Cascades in white sheets off the flashing,
Scatters itself with its own splashing.

1951

Rear Elevation

The blank back wall
Of the high white church
Stands broad and tall
Of clapboards each
Casting its thin
Horizontal strip
Of shadow within
White corner boards
And wide white frieze—
Stands private, stark
In blue sky or dark,
Through green or bare trees.

1977

Present Pasture

Pasture so various
With steeps precarious
And level lawns, and nooks
At the confluence of brooks—

No one can tell us why
We yearn, both ewe and I,
To quit these fair extents
For a future with no fence.

1951

Firstcomer

Beside the sleepless falls
Where broken waters pour,
He frames unquiet air
Within his four new walls
On top of his new floor—
Where none ever came before.

1960

The Notch of Light

That square notch under the bottom boughs
At the edge of the pinewoods on the hill
Is where I used to sit and still
Shall someday, keeping sheep or cows:
That notch of light that used to frame
My summer—let it stay the same
While I on other pastures browse.

1959

Strange Hands

When other hands work my contrivances,
Like this shed door I saved from falling off—
It shuts O.K. if you boost it with your knee—
The way I treat it, it'll last forever;
A person that demands smooth operation
Will have it on his head before breakfast.
Strange hands don't make the same allowances.

1961

The Start

Tired workmen will survey
The labor of their day:

These stones that moved so slow
Begin to make a row;

Tomorrow night you'll see
What they intend to be.

1951

Trick Back

The man with a trick back
Anticipates attack:

See him one minute big
And strong to lift and dig,

The next laid low, in knots—
This man has second thoughts.

1970

What Are You Going to Do Today?

"What are you going to do today?"
I'd ask my neighbor and he'd say,
"Pile up what I did yesterday."
He seldom said more than he had to.

Nor did he always mean split wood.
In principle he understood
What matters is what's put away:
What counts is what there is to add to.

1959

Handyman

His lifetime as town handyman—
Building & General Repairs,
Attendance at all chimney fires—
Has made his mind a working plan
Of everybody's halls and stairs.

1951

Dry Noon

Their low house nooning in the maple shade,
The pair inside remember having hayed.

The day today is dry and very fine—
Good haying weather, he has said, yes sir—
He who will hay no more, come rain or shine.

In all the valley, not a breeze to stir
The old man's breeches drying on the line.

1957

A *Pair of Georgics*

THE FEED ROOM

The feed room on my farm
Has a fine civil charm,
With everything I use
In order ranged about:
The bins for storing feed,
Lidded against the greed
Of creatures on the loose,
The scoop to serve it out,
The feed-pans of bright tin,
The shelf for medicine
(Bag Balm and soothing talc),
The scale for measuring
The daily yield of milk
(Subtracting weight of pail),
The wall-chart with the date,
Name of the milker, weight,
The pencil on a string
Suspended from a nail,
The broom to sweep the floor,
The button-fastened door.

What civilization means
Is nothing more abstruse
Than having the right machines
At hand and fit for use.

1954

LECTURE BY THE PROFESSOR OF PASTORAL CARE

Let's take for an instance
My nanny named Constance,
Dear Constance my goat
(Quote Connie unquote):

She caught a hind hoof
In the slats of her stall

126

And raised the barn roof
With her baritone yammer
Till I came with my hammer
And pinch-bar and all,
And got her foot freed
And rubbed her sore shin
And pronounced her as fine
As she'd ever been.

But she went off her feed
And lost her bright eye,
Began to get thin
And almost went dry—
A full-fledged decline.
I couldn't think why.

She favored that foot
As though it still hurt
But I couldn't find
A thing, except dirt—
No break in the skin,
No swelling, no bruise.
It couldn't be rot.
But I bathed it and put
On an ointment I use.

And still she declined.
I finally thought,
It must be her mind—
She's afraid of that slit—
It'll catch her again.
I gave her a pen
With a solid plank floor.
By George, that was it.
She's eating once more,
Her coat is like silk,
And she's up on her milk.

A body that's nervous
Requires psychic service.

1953

Summer Craft Fair

Amid their rich displays of knit
Or woven goods, enameled ware,
Stained glass, wood carving, pottery,
The proud embarrassed craftsmen sit
And look as if they didn't care
Whether we're sold on what we see.

I'm seeing how their winter's work
Made many a zero day and night
Important and serene and full.
Of course we ought to go beserk
And buy up everything in sight
To make our houses tenable.

1976

Behind the Wall

What shall we find behind this wall,
Only the room next door?
I never went in from here before.
Better stand by in case I call—

In case when I pry off this lath
We find a sealed staircase
Or someone's secret burial place,
Or even a charmed garden path—

A pocket of old night is all.
Wait; what's this down in the dark?
A carpenter's hammer old as the ark—
The hand long dead that let you fall.

1962

Repairing an Antique

Repairing an antique
That grew at last too weak
To bear its daily part,

I saved myself the price
Of a replacement twice
As strong but half as smart.

1976

Poplar Leaf

In each round poplar leaf
A poplar tree in brief—

An image in fine veins
Which every leaf contains

In abstract symmetry—
A green poem on the tree.

1981

Spiderweb

First prize for fine design?
The spiderweb wins mine.
But beauty's functional:

It makes it possible
For any gifted spinner
To taste fresh blood for dinner.

1982

Tree Roots

Tree roots without a sound
Probe, measure, pierce, surround
Obstacles underground;

Forced to go wide, go deep—
Forced out of normal shape—
They still provide upkeep.

1977

Beaver

This night construction crew
Creating swamp
To make your cellar damp
Without consulting you—

Suppose you breach their dams
And drain their ponds;
The colony absconds
By night, poor lambs,

With nothing but their brown
Impermeable pelts,
To locate somewhere else
Their cool exemplary town.

1979

Marks of Origin

Your pebble's an antique
Turned shapely, polished sleek
In ice-age gravel plants.

Your poems, like pebbles hard,
Are shaped and even scarred
By solid circumstance.

Where do hard wares begin?
These marks of origin
Remind us at a glance.

1978

Intending to Stop

The way she, hanging clothes,
Pursued him with her gaze
As down the road he sped
In the middle of the morning—
What was he to suppose—

That she dislikes her days
In the bend beside the river?
Himself, he comes and goes
Intending soon to stop
In some sweet place forever.

1957

Meeting of Lovers

Horns on the roads at close of day
As ruby taillights going away
Meet headlights coming with golden beam—
Meeting of lovers is night's theme.

Guitars tune up in dim cafes;
Stagelights will brighten soon on plays
As workday things give way to dreams—
Meeting and loving are night's themes.

1958

Showcase

At dusk your porch was your showcase
Where all the world could see your face
And tell that you were satisfied
To sit in a row in family pride.

Some you could name rode "out for the air"
To seek coarse pleasures off somewhere,
But you were visible in the gloaming
And sleeping long ere they were homing.

Not that they ever seemed to care.

1970

The Victorians at Dusk

To envy the Victorians at dusk
On cavernous verandas rocking, rocking

In recompense for the day's accomplished task,
And of their hopes of Heaven talking, talking,

One must forget this talking served to mask
A fear of Hell that now seems shocking, shocking.

1969

Night of the South Wind

About the barefoot pair
Seen striding with blown hair
Into their secret place
In the dark behind the school:

Let's say they strip and chase
Each other, snapping belts,
Then dressed pad somewhere else
To eat before they cool
Themselves in someone's pool
Or in the gathering shower
That'll break within the hour;

All night this is their town
To prowl in up and down,
To sport and laugh and leap
While the old owners sleep.

1972

Evening Ride

Dusk fades but does not blur:
In fact both birch and fir
Stand sharper than they were.

Through dusky countryside
Receding clarified
Forever let me ride.

1972

House-Chairs

House-chairs abroad at eve?
Somebody must believe
The spell these long days weave—
Perpetual afternoon—
Continues under moon.

1951

Evening Prayer

Would anybody come
If Evening Prayer were said?
Priest, choir, all Christendom
Apparently are dead

Who here in afterglow
Sang-in the summer night,
And often through dense snow
Trudged here to pray for light.

1975

Hymn 306

Had I become a priest
Seldom would I have ceased
From praying or at least

Kneeling
Under some holy ceiling . . .

As it is, I seldom rest
From writing hymns you hadn't guessed
Were hymns, the way they're dressed.

1978

Defunctive Music

Buried all through my music dictionary
Under the names of men I've never heard of
Are summaries of what they wrote: sad lists
Of symphonies, quartets, sonatas, songs,
Some of them, possibly, not ever published;
Some, probably, not ever even heard;
Few, certainly, about to be performed—
Like Etienne Mehul's opera *Joseph**
Or a cantata by N. Zingarelli**—
Creations that have only this much life.

*1807
**1829

1982

135

Chamber Music

Piano, cello, violin—
You dialogs of instruments—
One of the civilized events
Is your consenting to begin
Bringing your boundless moments in.

1975

Manual III

Even as I celebrate
My long experience
With manuals Swell, Great,
And their sweet difference,
I long to go one higher
To Swell, Great, Choir.

This Manual III
With its own stops and couplers—
Think what a gain—
Like adding Italy
With its expanse
Of plains and poplars
To Spain
And France.

This having three
Instead of two
Places to be
Would mean no more
Choosing just either/or:
Would in effect give twice
The choice.

1977

My Instruments

Twelve stops and seven ranks—
Organ was once my wonder:
My pedals and key-banks
Performed orchestral jobs
And spoke with a lush thunder
When I drew all the knobs.

Piano soon came back
As my first instrument:
Whatever it might lack
In blast and simulation
It freed me to invent.
Thank God for limitation.

1966

Canned Brahms

Perfection guaranteed,
Canned Brahms can't *not* succeed.

But neither can the groove
Allow it to improve:

All it can do is play
Forever the same way,

Lacking the joy and terror
Of risking public error.

1950

Control

Control is in the weight
The player focuses
On each successive finger:

To see each key struck straight
In rippling passages,
In flying he must linger.

1950

The Difference

All music from this "school"
Seems made by the same rule,
Like ribbon from one spool.

Thank God poems have the sense
To keep a difference;
The difference *is* sense.

1975

Full Moon

Empurpling the near sky
With its hot golden dye,

The moon stays up all night
By varying its height

Luxuriously slow
From low to high to low,

And only after dawn
Discolors and is gone.

1979

Indian Summer

I
This spell of golden weather
Holding twelve days together—

What do you do with riches?
Spend. The only hitch is

The knowing that no giver
Can hand out gold forever.

II
O row of golden days
Dawn still in silver haze;

Go slowly on and on
And suddenly be gone.

III
Bleached golden lie
Our uplands in pure sky,
Long surfeited with summer
And waiting but to die:
Come winter, you slow-comer.

1975, 1976, 1979

Harvesting the Squash

Among the great surprises
Is harvesting the squash:
When I pull up my vines
I marvel at what rises
Out of dense leaves, weeds, grass:
Squashes unseen till now,
All different shapes and sizes,
All worthy to win prizes.

1975

The Cold Hotel

A closet door stood at the window pane
As late sun streaked the mountainside through rain—
The summer gone would never come again.

The mountain, though, would stay the winter through,
Even with no one to admire the view
While waiting for the dinner bell.

And both were real—the hollow cold hotel
So lonely present, and those absent far
It could not call again from where they are.

1951

At the Crossing

In half an hour there'll be a freight
Splitting the night at a downhill rate.

Hard work to credit such an event,
The quiet seems so permanent.

I like it dark, I like it quiet,
Though neither does for a steady diet—

They're on the way at their downhill rate—
What'll we talk about while we wait?

1957

Between the Rails

The flower between the rails
Where downbound freight trains roll
Lives inches from disaster
In turbulence and quakes:
Inches are all it takes.

1980

The Yellow Lampshade

Stripped are the dooryard trees,
Raking and burning done,
And what the traveler sees

In the low noonday sun
That keeps the housefront warm
Is where the lampshade basks.

From blizzard and civil storm
Is a living room safely won?
The traveler hopes, but asks.

1948

Anniversary Posy

Shopping the whole fair through
For something nice for you
At, say, a dollar or two,
I found the poet's booth
Handles the cheapest truth:
How will this posy do,
In memory of our youth?

1951

Fall Dance

Now that our colleges are keeping,
The city teems with couples in pants
Who either will or won't be sleeping
Together after this night's dance.

In either case they take a chance—
Of saving what was not worth keeping,
Or starting what may end in weeping—
They leave it well to happenstance.

1966

To a Speaker

Right after you begin
We'll know what shape we're in

By who you think you are
And what you take us for.

Not that you'll have to say—
We'll read you anyway.

1978

One Fall Day

One fall day of high color and high wind
The trees will glitter on a hundred hills
As all their leaves, their longest journey starting,
Reserve their bravest gesture for departing.

1966

The Wind

That day the wind was busy in the sky
Children who heard or felt it posting by
Marveled how it could go at such a pace
All day in one direction past one place.

1951

Horse in Pasture

All fall the farm horse at the bars
Just stands, not watching the passing cars,
Not moving his eyes across the view,
Not even—unlike the cattle—feeding.
Poor horse, I say; nothing to do,
Like knitting or whittling, rocking, reading.

1962

Nothing to Do

Still day, late fall;
Low cloud encloses all,
Gray ceiling and gray wall.
The sawmill's whine is muffled.

No wind comes sporting by;
There are no leaves on high
To rush if they were ruffled.

Her last defenses down,
Earth has no business of her own
But waits the pleasure of the sky.

Nothing to do but wait and see
If rain it be
In a chilly douse,

Or snow, the season's first
At midnight when we aren't around
Gaining upon the ground
Where summer lies dispersed—

Soon we shall waken in a snow-lit house.

1949

Pasture Puddles

Days when the pasture land
In rain lets the white sky
Into the watery ground,
I step where heavens lie
Below me all around.

1970

November View

In view of all the veiled white days
And long black nights to be lived through

With only monthly P.T.A.'s
And Grange-nights to look forward to—

To keep November from stopping its life
Seems almost more than our town can do.

1964

Beyond the Death of Roses

My season doesn't close
Because the summer closes:
My household flower blows
Beyond the death of roses,
And even in deep snows
When the cold oak tree dozes
Consoles me and composes.

1969

Material Beauty

Material beauty being beyond my means,
I made with words on paper some few scenes—
Interiors, landscapes in both whites and greens—

To give at least my thoughts rich housing,
Not only in their sessions of carousing
But in their intervals of rest and drowsing.

1969

Prelude To

Still the worst blasphemy that we commit
Is treating any time as prelude to:

Day as the time before we close and quit,
Night as the time before we rise and do.

Be out in loving care till day goes west;
Then in, to inward love of dark and rest.

1957

Lively Places

Living apart, I read of lively places,
Evoking by my window stylish faces

Whose nods and frowns electrify large rooms
And speed men toward their fortunes or their dooms—

Then shut the book and keep my own country
Where the rule is no one loses except me.

1969

Skyway

Back farm at the end of earth
Without access by highway,
Know that they know your worth,
And have devised a skyway:

146

Just open your walls to wires
And let their last appliance
Bring you a world of liars
Caught in the act by science.

1951

Book Review

Has he developed as a writer—
Grown better as his hair grew whiter?

Not really, early work aside;
He's stayed much the same since he hit his stride.

But knowing what age can do to verse,
Let's praise him for not growing worse.

1969

The Risk with Any Voice

You run the risk with any voice
That anything it sings
Will sound too much like the other things.
You could restrict the choice
To, say, one high song and one low,
One fast, one slow,
One loud, one soft,
One smooth, one rough—
How few were few enough?

"What, limit song?" the voices scoffed.

1959

What a Poem Is

A poem is what you do about a fact—
A poem is an act.

A poem is what the mind does at its best—
Is an intelligence test.

A poem is a performance—on a stage
No larger than a page.

1957

Permanent Surprise

A *permanent* surprise?
Yes, what a poem supplies:

Unlike most jokes and stunts
Which seldom work but once,

The coil-springs of fine rhyme
Go off—ping—every time

Because it's not just wit,
Though wit is part of it;

The rest of it is heart,
The everlasting part.

1978

A Little Case

A poem's the essential novel
Housed in a little case:
The narrative compacted,
The hero a pronoun—
Two verbs tell how he acted.
The poem saves time and space.

1966

Reason for Rhyme

Let rhyme be your defense
From too much reason in the choice
Of words: let happy accidents
Surprise your sense
And please your voice.

1963

Mason's Trick

From masons laying up brick
To build a rosy wall
Level and square and tall,

We borrow a mason's trick,
Or at least a builder's term:
Rhymes keep our corners firm.

1967

149

Publication

The joy of publication
Is thinking how your words
Have taken flight like birds
Out of this isolation
To perch awhile on stands,
Be held awhile by hands,
In far parts of the nation.

1954

The Next Book

May the next book you read
Be what you need—

A pocket universe
Ample yet terse,

And offering connections
In all directions.

1969

Revelations

Of course if we didn't write,
Our faults wouldn't come to light.
As for our virtues, they
Are what our writing earned—
We carry them away:
The poem's what the poet learned.

1961

Out of the Money

Out of the money which
Causes the rich,

I stay friends with the poor,
Whom I write for.

1971

Testifying

Why, if the world is dying,
Why must I, crying,
Keep testifying?

My sense that all is lost
Can't quite defeat my trust
That all will last.

1971

Being Old

I hated being young
With nothing seen or sung.

No one likes feeling weak
Or looking so antique,

But I love being old
With something seen and told.

1978

The Trouble with Me

I may have double
The usual trouble
In consequence of
Dividing my love.
No, no, not two wives;
What I mean is two lives.
Since poets aren't paid
I'm also in trade:
I teach school for pay.
I'm kidding, you say?
No, I don't make jokes
About my young folks.
I give them my best
And count myself blessed
To be of some use
In the world's working day.
There's still time to write
Poems by night.
One lucky enough
To be teacher *and* bard
Had better work hard
And try to produce
Some tolerable stuff.

1958

The After-Life

In *my* play on the after-life
(And this should save my having to write it)
The entire cast of characters
Would wear their tombstones on their backs:

See the assorted obelisks,
Crosses, angels, mausoleums
(All papier maché, of course)
Reading each other's middle names . . .

The happiest person in the lot?
The unknown, with the unmarked grave.

1962

Private Practice

Men of the great world being required
To give up private practice
Are only seen in public attired
In rightness retroactive.

While elsewhere, privately admired
And fallibly productive,
Great men of the world cannot be hired
To give up private practice.

1965

Holy Place

Brothers who every hour
Give thanks for sun or shower
And a holy place as well,
As bidden by the bell
In the square central tower—
Your thanks give you a power.

1983

Under the Holy Eye

The world and I when young
And backward and content
Were visible among
The several bodies hung
About the firmament

Under the holy eye.
Though we all strove alone,
Some cloistered behind stone,
Some under the wide sky,
Our struggles yet were known,

Our Bibles still were true.
Then everything proved vast,
And numerous, and fast,
And, Father, either you
Or we flew out of view.

1959

The Qualities of Saint

The qualities of saint
Grow every day more quaint:
Simplicity and silence
Seem all too fine and faint
Weighed against wealth and violence;
Serenity and prayer
Which like the hermit's herb
Draw nurture from the ground
Are not at home in the air
At speeds surpassing sound.

Fast is no more a verb
But a soft adjective
Employed in every blurb
That fabricates false need.

154

You saints who love to live,
Better get used to speed—
A mile a second? More,
Yea, multiples thereof—
And luxury, and war.
What if you live to love?

1954

The Wet and the Dark

This rain's no inconvenience to the beaver,
But makes tame cattle huddle at the gate;
I too have been as much at home in the river
As in this thin air where we stand and wait.

This dark's no disadvantage to the cat,
But makes tame people huddle by the fire;
I too've gone prowling through the liquid black
In company with old sweet damned desire.

1961

Between Here and There

The highway between here and there
Is where we hurry, hoping
There'll be no need of stopping
For lack of oil or air,
Water, or gasoline—
The country is so bare,
The lights so few and far between
That side of here, this side of there.

1954

The Busy Town

At sundown then my mother and I
Walked with the wind along the street;
The sky was red in front of us,
The cold snow creaked beneath our feet.

When we at last arrived downtown
Some people talked with us and I
Looked into lighted windows full
Of clocks and rugs and toys to buy.

Too soon we turned back to the long
Dark street and faced into the wind;
Someone creaked past us, hurrying down
To join the throng before it thinned.

1933

Short Hill

Time for supper, and still
You're sliding on the hill
I should have thought too short
To give you so much sport.
But then, I've lost the art
Of driving fast machines
Great journeys through small scenes.

1969

Reflections from a Pail

When on a zero noon
Sun's at the window flashing
Reflections from a pail
You carry to the barn,

Let yellow ripples lapping
All round you on dull matter
Beguile you for a sail
Upon a summer water.

1951

Sun in Winter

More welcome in the house in these short days
Than at any other season is the sun,
Who yellows now the walls of our south rooms
And gilds the bubbles of steam-beaded bowls
On kitchen tables, while outdoors the eaves
Slow raining sunlit drops, and down the track
An engine idling, warm the winter noon.

1936

Full Tanks

I owe the company such a sum
I hate to see the oil truck come,
But here it is, and the street is blurred
With more snow coming to join the banks
Along the drive. It would be absurd
Not to feel thankful for full tanks
With winter continuing so grim.
As for the driver, it's nothing to him
How much I owe—so fetch out the kettle
To pour on the cap and expand the metal,
And, each of us keeping an eye on the meter,
Rehearse all the virtues of oil as a heater.

1952

Love of Snow

In those years, days like this
When storm made the oak leaves hiss
Were days of winter bliss:

Pulling our sleds to the top
Of town where houses stop
And fields and pastures drop

Over back to farms and the river,
We'd slide and climb forever—
Till first dark made us shiver;

Then homeward tired and slow,
Ready for kitchen glow,
All white from love of snow.

1950

January Night

The shiny trodden snow
In harsh illumination,
So cold your bootsoles creak;
The houses double-glassed
Against the searching blast—
These things you may have classed
Under the heading, Bleak.

Fact is, the snow was trod
By people warmly shod
And coated—none in mink—
Sashaying to and fro
Betwixt the stores, the station,
Tavern, and house of God,
And this bright, crowded rink.

1954

Zero Night

Keep our three fires this zero night—
The kitchen, front-room, upstairs fires—
And keep in hand all pipes and wires
In the dark house while we sleep tight
Under the quilted roof moon-white.

1962

In the Store

Slight seedy sir with woodsy tread
Now watching women buying bread,

We gather from your very stance
How you enjoy a Grange-hall dance.

No settlement of any size
But has a sport whose saucy eyes

Defy some sulky local belle
To try the backwoods trail to hell.

1952

Earthquake

Because I never felt earth quake
I think of her as something like
A well-built house on solid footings.

Whereas in fact she's a flying machine
Whose primitive boiler seethes unseen
Under constantly crumbling gratings.

1965

Two Old Gents

Two old gents standing nose to nose
Are generally engaged in talk;
I see with something of a shock
These are about to come to blows.

It may be they won't hurt each other,
It would hurt me to watch them tussle.
Youth is the time for a show of muscle—
Which may be stopped by someone's mother.

1953

Time to Plant Trees

Time to plant trees is when you're young
So you will have them to walk among—

So, aging, you can walk in shade
That you and time together made.

1970

Away

Away from home be cool—
Or taken for a fool.

Home is the kindly place
Where no one minds your face.

1950

Going a Long Journey

for Eunice Young Craig

I know what things to pack,
But what to leave to you
In case I don't come back—
And then, what if I do?
I wish one of us knew.

This life is done the day
I lock that door and go:
Till then we have to play
We don't know what we know—
And know what we don't know.

1976

Flying

You have to trust the brain
That engineered this plane—
He's our best engineer.

Yes, but your second-best
Had *his* chance to suggest
Cheapening every gear.

1966

The Gothic Builders

My idea of accomplishment?
Like what the Gothic builders did:

Sink stone on stone to reach a depth,
Set stone by stone to reach a length,
Raise stone on stone to reach a height
With window-walls to let in light
And, buttressed, bear the thrust
Of soaring vaults;
Then top the whole with tall square towers.

All faiths may have some faults,
But their accomplishment for theirs
Dwarfs ours for ours.

1964

The Transept

The strong high-stepping march
Of columns bearing vaults
Along the side-aisle halts
In the view up through this arch

To the transept gallery:
Vaulting already tall
Gives on a taller wall
Where the builders crossed their T

In the way then specified
To give the eye a ride.

1975

The Polypody

The idea of the Gothic vault
Is in the polypody fern
Which springs from a clustered base
In flaring arcs
With vertical and transverse ribs.

When the Gothic builders set about
Paving the steep
Highdrive to Heaven with curved
And fitted stone, their first blueprint
Was this green pattern in the woods.

1964

Belfry

for Garret Keizer

A town should have a tower
And on the tower a clock
And in the tower a bell
Chiming each quarter-hour
To notify the flock
That everything is well,

Especially at night
When somebody seems bound
To suffer dislocation;
That's when a handmade height
Letting down quiet sound
Can uphold civilization.

1975

If I Could Draw

If only I could draw
I'd show you what I saw
This morning in the street:
Postures of hands and feet
And abdomen and seat
That hide or do not hide
What's happening inside.

1967

Old Fellow

Mouth open, the old fellow sleeps in the sun
On the tired bench that spans the polished granite
Corner of the monument in the city park.
If the bench should give way, he'd be cut in two . . .
What bothers us most about him, though, in passing,
Is the idea that he's not well connected:
Homeless, no doubt, and churchless, collegeless—
It may be even lawless—can it be
He's so far gone as to care nothing for
All that these institutions codify?
To think of anyone letting the future come
Upon him as it wills, unfiltered through
The bronze grille of the First National Bank!

1942

The Buildings at Charlottesville

Mr. Jefferson's classic
Red and white facades
Govern his green lawns,
His blue air and mountains.
Nature could seem careless;
He was to take pains.
Mind he had and means
To keep making order
Out of brick and wood,
Out of word and law.
This was where he lived,
This good governor,
Man of law and brick,
Man of word and wood.

1963

First Things

Before there was a wider, this was wide,
This water that I once more walk beside.

Before there was a higher, this was high,
This grove that filters green light to the eye.

This is the story of first things—each one
A perfect joy before comparison.

1955

For Robert Frost

Forty new poems of yours to read!
This was like being given deed
To a new house with forty rooms,
Each being a new place to live
At first till our own life resumes,
And evermore a place to come
And find you making us at home—
Few men have had houses to give.

1963

Frost at Bread Loaf

Already in himself a force of Nature,
The white-maned mountain lion of a poet
Who's had the queer luck to be lionized
Advances as a cloud across the landscape
To win another conversation with
The college poetry establishment.

1969

Looking for Happiness

Where are we to begin
Looking for happiness?
At every known address:
Is anyone glad within—
About new love or money?
Being released from pain?
Still waiting for the train
To the land of milk and honey?

1976

New Poems

Secure in Summer

Secure in summer once,
Just let yourself exult,
Declining like a dunce
To act like an adult
Forseeing consequence
And reckoning result.

1984

The Long Summer

Then summer sat and smiled
As though to stay all year,
But then I was a child.

Now, given to good cheer
And glad to be beguiled,
I stay a child all year.

1966

The Water-Meadows

The low end of the lake,
Half water and half sky,
Where water-meadows lie

With little need of fence
Since shoreline on one side
Defines circumference,

Sees light pour evenly
Over the level scene,
Half landscape, half marine.

1985

Hay-Jumpers

When hay was put in loose,
We jumpers had our use:
We packed the stuff away.

Climbing the side of the bay
To a high ledge, we'd stand,
Each pick his place to land,
Then soar off into space
And plunge up to his face
In the sweet springy stuff.

By noon we'd had enough.
The jumping was pure play
But breathing chaff in the murk
Was quite a lot like work
On a blue-and-gold hay day.

1953

Swimmers

Eye-level with the lake,
Skimmers of deeps opaque
See green steeps take
Ascent from the water line,
And in long sweeps combine
Bright birch and dusky pine.

1951

Haying Moon

The moon was up before the sun went down:
Out of a thunder-head it rolled, huge orange,
Over the vacant yellow stubble-field—
Vacant except for a tractor and two haycarts
Now idly representing hot noon labor.

1968

High Meadow

Tonight in the high meadow they're still haying
In the perfect weather for which they've been praying.

With truck and tractor headlights on high beam
Making the landscape unreal as a dream,

They're getting in a well-cured bumper crop;
When haying's this good, no one wants to stop.

1969

The Open Shed

A boy too valley-bred
To sit in an open shed
At a farmhouse on a height
With valleys left and right
While lightning grazed the place,
I came near losing face.
My elders sat unscared—
Think how long they'd been spared!

1969

High Farm

At the head of the field stood house and barn
On a rocky shelf already high;
At the head of the pasture stood the sky.

The whole place sloped to a valley view
Mostly of firwoods with a few
Farms and the point of the village spire.

"My grandfather built with his own lumber.
Look here in the mow—how's that for a timber?
We're framed to weather polar blasts.

"We're also neighbor to the sun,
And grow a good part of our staples:
Beef, apples, sugar from our maples.

"We're far from governments and crowds,
But near to stars and winds and clouds—
The sky's our principal institution."

1963

Hill or Valley

Hill farm or valley farm—
If choosing just on charm,
Where would you rather be?

High liver or low liver—
Some mountains or a river—
Which would you rather see?

1966

172

Fern

Aroma of bruised fern
I smelled while berrying
This noon in a hot gully

Reminded me how fern
Was once my covering
When hiding from a bully.

1969

Dooryard/Dirt Road

Our dooryard came right down
To the dirt road from town;
Both shady, neither wide,
They lived there side by side,
One grassy, one bare brown,
With nothing to divide
Them but the line, still loose,
Of private/public use.

1954

Local Love

Where I grew up, great buildings
Were things to think about
And look at pictures of,
But never expect to see.

Home was our place to be,
Involved in local love
For our land and our house,
Belonging to our holdings.

1965

The Lay of Your Land

I tell how you stand
By the lay of your land:

Your dominant hill
Is well-shaped or ill,

Your covering sky
Low-posted or high;

The slant of your yard
Spells easy or hard,

And the light on your door
Says thrive or go poor.

1966

Lost Streets

Along the boughs in darkling woods
The fireflies form neighborhoods
Whose strings of lights evoke lost streets

Where we unpacked our worldly goods
And slept and woke between the sheets,
And tasted comforts and defeats.

1985

Lost for Good

The lapsed road lost in the wood,
All pierced by brush and weeds,
Where no car speeds,

Is not more lost for good
Than busy tar or gravel
We never travel.

1950

Rising at Two in June

Oh look—on the shiny floor:
I said old mother moon
Would find our open door
That lets in the loud loon
Who laughs in the mist by the shore.

Now's her high lunar noon
When she'll be keeping bright
The latter end of night
For the late, or early, goer—
She'll get me headed right.

Soon father sun, at four.

1965

Moonset

Moon down at the end of Main Street
Where the land westward drops
To sidings where the trains meet,

How close you stand to stare
Into deserted shops
Around the vacant square.

1975

Summer Is Swift

Summer is swift and turns not back.
Sequence of berries is straw, rasp, blue, and black;
Of minor field-life, hyla, firefly, locust.
In each a two-weeks age is focused.

1952

Chore-Time

Life being an affair
Of moving something square
From here to there,

Quite often in a hustle,
Most burdens that we bear
Are borne by muscle.

1968

The Roof

This flatly ineffectual roof
I patch up after every storm
Lies here as perfect proof
Its builder had not mastered form.

Nor did he care much for my time
In giving me this cause to climb
Perpetually and potter—
A roof incapable of water!

1952

Cement

How good of someone to invent
This flowing form-stopped element
That hardens now to permanent
To give my barn a new basement—

And elsewhere on the continent
Helps hold up even government.

1974

Idle Hound

As an idle hound busily lopes all over,
Through fences, up a field, across a yard,
Along the highway home, with springy gait,
Tail swinging, ears a-flop: so I as lover
Of this terrain and people, local bard,
Busily saunter round and speculate.

1950

General Cram and Bishop Butterfield

By General Cram* and Bishop Butterfield**,
Both friends of mine when young, I stand revealed
As the idle fellow that I really am:

Civilian Layman Hayford as I'm called,
I never have amounted to a damn,
Compared, at least, to Butterfield and Cram.

 *Maj. Gen. Reginald M. Cram, Vermont Adjutant General from 1967
  to 1981
**Rt. Rev. Harvey D. Butterfield, Bishop of Vermont from 1961 to 1974

1976

Reading My Poems at My 50th

I brought my trophies with me
To give out free
To mates who'd made *their* fortunes
Differently.

1985

Cross-Country

Of all the events, you enter one—
Cross-country against oblivion;
Stake heart and lungs on that long gamble,
Set off at what appears an amble,
Certain you'll never know you've won.

1949

Far and Fair

Ever the heart is smitten
With what is far and fair,
Unlearned yet unforgotten.

Always we long to hear
The tune no one has written,
Authentic, wild, and clear.

1951

Delivering a Poem

You slip in past his guard,
Hit him exactly square
And adequately hard,
And get right out of there.

1951

Words

Words are condensed experience:
One way to be absurd
Is treat a word
As easy eloquence.

1950

The Diffy-Cult

This being difficult
In a work of art
For difficulty's sake—

What surer way to insult
The serious heart,
Which never learned to fake.

1968

Almost Perfect

The poem either works or does not work;
If not, it might as well miss by a mile.

The poet figures either as God's clerk
Or as a clumsy juvenile.

One might produce an almost-perfect poem,
But that's an almost-contradictory term.

1985

Plain

The word for me is plain:
Plain not too beautiful,
Plain comprehensible.

Embroidery and gush
And beating round the bush
All go against my grain.

1974

Making Form

North-born, I worked at form
In order to keep warm.

I wouldn't fall apart
In art or out of art;

Whatever got my goat
I bore instead of wrote.

Others were more profound,
Some worked so deep they drowned.

But I'm still making form
In storm and out of storm.

1968

Still Life

Four apples and a knife
On a ground of violet plush
Along with a glass of water.

The purpose of still life:
To see how much your brush
Can make of little matter.

1978

Before the Flood

Before the flood of pleasure, ease was rare;
Adults had neither time nor money to spare
Except once yearly, maybe, at the fair.

In rooms kept always orderly and clean
Children found out quite soon what fathers mean
When they declare, "Children are to be seen . . ."

School was the day's containment in a cage
With women whose authority was age,
And older boys powered by an older rage.

How glad some of us were at the first signs
Of thawing in a few long-frozen lines—
Small freedoms taken, unbendings of spines:

More colored pictures in the magazines,
More curving surfaces on new machines,
Less Greek and math required by college deans . . .

Or did this whole thing start when some preferred,
To fifths and unisons, the sixth and third—
Lush "discords" at which Grecian minds demurred?

Whoever loosed it, has the flood of pleasure
Rubbed the sharp edges off both work and leisure
And left us nothing difficult to treasure?

1959

182

River Music

Following as in a dream
The long fall of a stream
Downward indefinitely,
The music meets the sea
In a quarter of an hour—
Unnaturally short.
Even the amplest art
Condenses natural power.

1969

To Sing

To sing is in fact to learn:
The cry which has to start
As trouble in the heart
Whose function is to yearn
Will then enlist the mind
To make—a happy find.

And as this news takes shape
And makes good its escape
Out to the world of affairs
Where clerks and millionaires
Regarding it—agree,
To sing is indeed to be.

1951

Mechanic

Acquainted in my engine
As I am in my book,
He knows right where to look
For that which all things hinge on
And what it's apt to hook
To and impinge on—
There he lies whistling, curled.
To each his underworld.

1950

Playboy

Your poet is the boy
Who makes the world his toy
By phrasing for his time
In words that run and rhyme
Some of the riddles deep
That have disturbed men's sleep—
At play with consonant letters!
A problem to his betters.

1951

A Run of Luck

During a run of luck
My thinking runs amok:

I start to think it's meant,
Instead of accident.

Lucky I never had
Luck enough to run quite mad.

1976

Money and Fame

Never let me let money
Or fame go to my head—

Nothing we need to dread;

I'd make myself look funny
Counting it merited.

1977

The Danger of Literary Success

Once people start to praise
Your every turn of phrase
Simply because it's you
And not because it's true,
You're out of things to do.

1981

Having to Be First

This having to be first
Whenever you compete
Even if you have to cheat
Must be an awful thirst.

Seeing someone must be last,
I reckon why not me;
Call this my gift to the
Unwillingly surpassed.

1965

My Lost Chance

If poetry hadn't got me when it did
I might have been a parson and lived amid
The faithful as a good man at my prayers
In minor parsonages with peeling stairs.
There I'd have been considered *justly* meek
Or been accepted as a *harmless* freak,
And there if something happened to my calm
I could have taken refuge in a psalm
Out of my memory or off a shelf,
And not have had to make one up myself.

1962

Two Basic Facts

I
Poets are who is glad
When anyone is having
The best time to be had.

II
The saddest fact I know
Is that tranquility
Is neglect of others' woe.

1967 and 1950

Immortal Child

Once soundly brought to birth
Kicking and drawing breath,

Your poem unlike its maker
May live still fresh forever

186

Whether in open day
Or somewhere tucked away—

And should your name drop off it
May even profit.

1977

Unified Field Theory

To my poor no-math mind
The world seems so designed

That one simple equation
Should cover all Creation:

Impersonal and blind
May almost equal kind.

1979

Dead Language

Saying meter and rhyme
Have outlived their time
And should be called dead

Is like saying English
Is dead as a language
Because all is said.

1985

Lost Works

How many men have written
Works that have not survived.
The world has been deprived
Of matter great or small—
Not that size really matters:
We need all sizes, all.

1961

Confrontation

Their backs to civilization,
A few uniquely candid
Maintain a confrontation
With data bare and splendid;

On their deserted path,
The doubts the rest reject
To spare the intellect
Are theirs to wrestle with.

1950

My Last Defeat

Living up here apart
In this high hidden retreat
After my last defeat,
I've plied my ancient art
And on the whole downplayed
My classic unrealized
Wish to be recognized—
For the friends this might have made.

1970

Writer's Joy

Some joy of a forgotten day
Stands at my elbow, dim;
My morrow's joy will be to pay
My compliments to him.

1950

Haunted

Haunted we are by the love of God
Which plays as music round us
To move us and astound us
And yet *be* moved to find us awed.

1950

Your Poem

Your poem once it has left your hands
Is anyone's who understands:

A reader reading his very plight—
How did you ever get it right?

And now, if you dare alter it
He's hurt; it *was* his favorite.

1971

My Inch

You who will come to judge me
I pray may not begrudge me
My inch upon your shelves,
But yield me, as yourselves
Aspire to be served,
This point at which I stand
As on a spectral band
In high heaven hugely curved,
Point after infinite point
To infinite rays conjoint,
Each ray a street to enter
The world and tap its center,
Each point a frail distinction
Against time and extinction.

1949

Pruning the Tomatoes in August

Time grows
Who knows
How short:
Crop tops
And leaves—
Even blossoms
Are surplus parts—
So sun
And rain
Can get
To roots,
And fruit
Now set.
Too late
To wait
For starts.

1977

Cool Rain

This cool rain on the corn
Which suffered so long dry
Under the hot July—
Too much for one old man
To water with a can—
Will leave us all reborn.

1979

Water

Water although weak food
Nevertheless is good:

Solid or melted ice
Helps make the hot days nice,

And steaming cups of tea
Keep winter company.

But principally water,
As days turn colder, hotter,

Is known for quenching thirst,
Which though not mentioned first

Is not an hour younger
Than its companion hunger.

1952

Absences

No robins on the lawn,
No singing in the trees
Though green leaves still are on—

It's absences like these
And silences at dawn
Persuade us summer's gone.

1987

Our Robins

I pitied in my youth
Our robins faring south
From their familiar homes
To take whatever comes.
Of course they know from birth
Their home address is Earth.

1987

The Seasons

So slow the seasons' change,
We follow their full range—
Beginning, middle, end;

Welcoming one and all—
Winter, spring, summer, fall—
Saying, So long, old friend.

1986

Summer's Promise

As soon believe in summer's promise
Of comforts effortless and cheap
As listen to the threat of winter
All efforts comfortless to keep:

My mind so short on merry truths
And long on melancholy reasons
Gathers itself again to weather
A revolution of the seasons.

1958

Fall Fair

Crowning our brief barbaric summer,
The great bulls with their golden balls
And the cows with their great bags
Come forth, though bored, to be admired.

While at the gate to the girly show
The dancers absently bounce their breasts
And the boys' crotches tighten—
And quite a lot of money changes hands.

1967

Fall Faculty Meeting

September, and we reconvene
From separations mountainous and marine,

Each hoping change has had the effect
Of sharpening the other's intellect.

1938

Father and Son

On those frequenting college lawns
The Founding Father frowns in bronze,
A hard man—hard enough for Son
To smash his empty bottle on.

1965

Sons

Most sons reject their fathers' shibboleths
And suffer pleasure in their fathers' deaths.

1978

Light

Be light on your feet:
Your prints exact
Step evenly from fact to fact—
Be light, be neat.

Let light in your eyes:
Look where the sun cures hay.
Like water under open day
Be clear—grow wise.

Light fire to greet
All whom bad weather
Brings in to hope awhile together—
Give light, give heat.

1946

A Beaten Man

Defy your father and defeat him;
He can't very well fight back
Without commencing an attack—
He'd rather let you beat him.

However, once you've disobeyed him,
You may not relish what you've made him.

1987

Partisan

Dispense with all belief
Except in God and man
Lest as a partisan
You come to calling thief
Whoever slights your chief.

1950

Two-Party System

Republicans or Democrats
Stealing your homes or herds?

As soon teach cats
Not to catch birds—

Although most birds are not
As a rule so easily caught.

1979

The Same Old Drive

Cause of the coming war
Will be the very drive
That kept the race alive
Before—
The strongest one we've had:
The same old drive
That made us thrive
Has also made us bad.

1967

Redcoats

When soldiers all wore red
Some of them finally said
We're too easy to shoot,
And got a quieter suit
So no one knows they're there.
The enemy said No fair.

1987

In Company

In company too grave
I'm bound to misbehave.

In company too jolly
I'm often melancholy.

The world needs me, it seems,
To save it from extremes.

1953

What Future?

What future? said the boy;
You think we *won't* employ
Our power to destroy?

We haven't, since Japan.
You see no hope for man
In this? I think I can.

Maybe I'll change my mind.
But dad, most men are blind—
Why don't we lead mankind?

Son, if we found the route
To lead men in, some lout
Could also lead them out.

1953

Reflection on Man

Our sense may represent
The dear accomplishment
Of One not easily content,

One not disposed to flinch
From working, in a pinch,
In hundred-thousands of an inch,

Nor loath to share His stuff
For judging, fine or rough,
Too much, too little, and enough—

Thus fitting us for feats
Like letting sensual sweets
Make us what we call fools and cheats.

1952

The Good Brother

The brother of the Prodigal Son
Objecting that too much was done
About the Prodigal's return:
Fathers forgive what wastrels burn?
Let them pay good sons what they earn!

The son who never left his Lord
Should find this fact its own reward.
Of course. But folks go overboard
And reinstate the lost son found
Above the one who stayed around.

1967

Single Thought

Ye canons of this cathedral-church,
All old, distinguished men,
Authorities and authors, search
Your scriptures yet again
For texts that comprehend what ought
To be, and what we practice—
Verses that hold in single thought
Reality and justice.

1951

Two Bishops

The Bishop of Vermont is fond
Of his austere cathedral-church
And of his scattered faithful few:
He has to make a virtue out of Little.

The Bishop of New York is proud
Of his immense cathedral
(The largest in the world)
And of his many parishes, some rich:
He has to make a virtue out of Much.

1987

Notice to Employees

Young men much bigger than their jobs
Confront a quandary:
They either stretch vice-presidency
Or dwindle into snobs.

1950

Our Weight

Our weight works against us in most cases
Excepting as a fellow braces
His back against a post, or leans
Into his work; then is his person,
Which Heavenly Lightness laid a curse on,
For once no burden, but a means.

1954

Age Takes Too Long

Age takes too long to put on
To find with each new dawn
Some old importance lost.

Tell age forget the past—
Tell age things change so fast
Its teaching days are gone?

1965

Unsolicited

Men happy now will curse
The unsolicited future,

And even now rehearse
Anticipated torture.

1951

Our Youthful State

Too bad we all found out too late
The features of our youthful state
Should not have been embarrassments;

But when was ever girl or boy
In good position to enjoy
The gifts of hope and innocence?

1966

Free Spender

So much of summer gone—
How much I put off knowing;
Backward in coming on
Is brisk enough in going.

So let me spend each day
Like a twenty-dollar bill,
Till nothing's left to play
With, nothing in the till.

1959

One Day the Same Sweet Size

Days, metal tags just large
Enough to hold the date,
Drop from their skyhook straight
Into the waiting barge

That's towed out to discharge
Them yearly offshore, not
To liquefy or rot,
But linger as a scourge

To innocent navigation.
Dear Lord, economize:
One day the same sweet size
But sans enumeration,

Hung blank perennially,
Would show sound conservation,
Would leave the channel free—
Would cancel antiquation.

1950

Kindly Loosening

Old people may not hear the call
Of causes they once gave their all.

One gentle thing age does for the old
Is kindly loosening their hold.

So apples when they ripen fall.

1977

The Basis

That hope is all there is,
Basis of our great virtue
Courage, and that hope has
So slight a body and
Such wings to beat the hand—
This circumstance may hurt you
Until you understand
That it would not desert you,
But draw you to a land.

1950

Office

Is God indeed all mind,
No body, we should find
Him as our days less gaudy
Toward neatness are inclined:

As finally we gain
Daily the high terrain
Where is conducted gaily
The office of the brain.

1950

The Great Hope

Expanses and extents
Keep growing more immense
By adding small events . . .

What is at my command
Is this place where I stand
And this hour now in hand.

What I can do is grow
By using what I know
And learning as I go,

So at my death to be
All that was meant for me.
And then? We'll have to see.

The one great hope I own
Is that for having grown
We shall be told, Keep on.

1963

Short Sequence of Life and Death

1. Soft Assertion
Dawn soft asserts its claim
On him who holds it tame
To hide himself in covers
While he and light are lovers.

2. Lady
Her softly riotous garden
Days cross in luminous file
As though forewarned, no pardon
For any that dare be vile.

3. Our Roomer
Our roomer Night strolls up the hill
With the first star for a locket,
And I of sun have had my fill
And curl up in his pocket.

4. Waif
In principle a waif
In the large land abroad,
Man finds no proof that God
Even means him to be safe.

5. Curtain
The play acquires shape
Only as we are certain
It culminates in Curtain,
Which none alive escape.

6. Committal
The body when spirit is fled
Remains as a burdensome token,
And some must lament and be broken,
And some must bury the dead.

1950

The Bottle-Picker

Old man in any weather scavenging
What midnight automobile parties fling,
Whenever I pick you up with clanking sack
Slung by a shoulder-strap across your back,
Your paying public service seems to me
An answer to my fears of beggary:
Your way of earning pennies enough to dine
Exemplifies my own foreseen decline.

1956

Substance of Leaf

Like a stout woodland knoll
Where lightly leaf-shade lies,
Yet signifies
Substance of leaf,
So may your heart wear grief,
Shadow of soul.

1950

My Mother's Death at 91

Let her have pretty things
Now—no, not diamond rings
But, say, a china plate and cup
And, say, a silver spoon

To be her very own
For keeps now, not on loan,
To breakfast with when the sun comes up,
To sup with when the moon.

1968

For J.F.M.

What of the selfless case
Of one who leaves no trace
But his unselfish acts?

How to discern his face,
And how prolong his grace,
From such mute artifacts?

1950

Death by Drowning

for Nick Della Vecchia

The presence by my bed
Was of the one who drowned,
The only one I've lost
Elsewhere than on dry ground:

Must be you drowning-dead
Are chosen to accost
Sleepers who need advice
On doing something nice.

1988

The Single House

Few men in their old age are any use;
Instead of love they give and get abuse.

Nor does the world much notice when they're gone;
Exceptions sure, but nothing to count on.

And all of them go singly, though the grave
Is the single house in common they all have.

1969

Underlying

I shall be sorry to leave this earth
Where I have lived and died since birth.

But still a part of me will stay
To underlie a little hay—

My body worrisome and wayward
A spot of earth reaped by a hay-Ford.

1951

Always Free

Squirrels are always free
To leap from tree to tree
And every time connect,

Or any time descend
A trunk headfirst and end
This death-defying act.

1986

The Cardinal

The cardinal must know he shows
In winter woods all white and black;

He must see all the world as foes
And all day long expect attack.

Despite the cardinal's success,
I try for inconspicuousness.

1984

Hummingbird

At dark the hummingbird
Soft at my feeder heard
Filling his fuel tanks

Must shut his little mill
Down totally until
Daybreak. We both say thanks.

1988

Paleface

How pale my back and sides
Compared to horses' hides
Which may be black or bay,
Roan, chestnut, dapple-gray . . .
If asked I would have voted
To be as richly coated.

1985

Two Squirts

"In the eyes of a man of imagination, Nature is imagination itself."—William Blake

THE SKUNK

You talk about imagination—think:
A creature armed with nothing but a stink
Propelled to make aggressors stop and blink.

About his bad name as a dirty fighter,
Compared, say, to a scratcher or a biter,
You have to ask what makes it so much righter

To kill an enemy than make him cough
Just long enough so you can get clean off.

THE SQUID

The squid, more like the skunk than you might think,
Considering his home is in the drink,
Confounds his enemies by squirting ink.

About *his* ill fame as a dirty fighter,
Compared, say, to a Congressman or writer,
You have to ask why it's so much politer

To ruin an enemy than make him blink
Just long enough so you can rise or sink.

1964

Pulling Out All the Stops

No hearing the organ play
At services each week

Prepared me for the day
When first I heard it speak

With all the stops pulled out:
Lord, what a heavenly shout!

1987

The Old Organist

You few at Morning Prayer
Heard my sweet mix of string
And oboe which will sing
As long as I am there:
Some youngster should be found
Who'll learn to make this sound
While I am still around.

1973

After the Recital

What waits the artist after the recital,
A solo coffee in a night café?

As if anything but love could feed the vital
Hunger of one come home from worlds away.

1955

At the Party

How, resident in his fingers
Which now prop up his cheek
The power, sleeping, lingers
That made Beethoven speak.

1950

Night Shift

Outside the factory gates
In the parking lot in the rain
In the cold dark car she waits
For his lunch break at nine.

He's out, and off they roar,
But not for very long;
He'll be back on the floor
On time, or get in wrong.

They must be this week's lovers
And I must wish them well
On the glaring roads and rivers
Of this industrial hell.

1977

Thinly Closeted

Old couple snug abed,
Your window, early dark,
Flashed in my headlights' arc;

So thinly closeted
As so close by I sped,
You didn't blink, or hark?

1951

211

A *Pair of Couples*

I A BIT MORE DARK

"Me—anxious to be gone?
You want me still here at dawn?
Look at your clock. It's four—
Time I was out that door.
Wait, look how light it is.
Your neighbors have sharp eyes.
I'll wait now till the moon
Is set—it will be soon.
A bit more dark won't hurt.
Now, where'd I throw my skirt . . .

"All right, I won't dress yet.
Yes, one more cigarette.
Let's see your pillow. So.
Lean back and let's smoke slow.
Let's have *some* covers, dear—
All right, just up to here.
What are you, sort of tired?
You slept some. I've admired
Your knack of counting sheep
Right in the middle of—
What do we call it—love?

"You're asking will it last?
Of course not; it can't, past
A natural point. What then?
I'll have another man,
Of course. You get a woman.
Don't sit here and be sad.
Don't tell me you aren't human.
Shy maybe, but not narrow—
You wouldn't call this bad.
You want me back tomorrow—
Or should I say today—
Hey, that's just hours away!"

II AN ISLAND OFF THE CHART

"What do you say we start
For an island off the chart
Where our ideas of order
May for a while be safe
From accident and murder?"

"What now, you poor dear waif—
Where is there such an isle?"

"Dear wife, you needn't smile.
No, really now, I know
One, and know how to go."

"But look, it's winter, dear;
The children need us here.
And where'll we get the money?"

"It won't cost us a penny.
And we'll be nearer them
Than we are now—ahem."

"It won't be winter there?
What shall I need to wear?"

"Nothing—or something thin.
No winter where we're going—
Never the least wind blowing.
Go up and tuck them in.
I'll lower the thermostat—
You see, we'll *save* on that—
And tend to the lights and locks
Before somebody knocks.
By the time you've said your prayers
You'll hear me on the stairs.
Up there in the early dark
Our bed will be our bark."

1966

Each Other

They'd no idea what use
They might be to each other,

She still in her late youth,
He older than her father;

It seemed they had been left
Each other as a gift.

1983

The Girl

Gets right down to brass tacks,
Unbuttoning her breasts
And peeling off her slacks,
Remarking she detests,
In passing, Jews and blacks—
Proving a common cutie,
Dishonoring her beauty.

1978

Intruder

Intruder, you just left
Your shoe-print on my sill—
And an invaded feeling:

I had nothing worth stealing.
But articles of theft
Include good will.

1950

Held

Many securely held
In village unity
At one time once rebelled,
And came to know while free
The price of liberty.

1950

The Cost of Being What I Am

The cost of being what I am is high
In comfortable certainties foregone:
I cannot say for certain that the sky
Is Heaven, nor that a bearded God looks on;

I cannot claim the damages I cause
Are justified by my unworldly ways,
Though I am surer than I ever was
That what I celebrate deserves my praise.

When you, aloft, my namesake and my son,
Attempt the balances that are my art,
I see my penitence has just begun
For having failed to teach you safer sport.

I didn't know the bargain that I made
Would bring this heavy reckoning to be paid.

1954

Son

The boy no longer child
But open-faced and mild
Makes such speed as he can
Toward putting on the man.

1950

Assistant Secretary

My father finally could sign himself
Floyd W. Hayford, Assistant Secretary.
His middle name was Wilbur, after *his* father,
Wilbur Elroy—W.E. Hayford.
Grampa failed as butcher several times
By trusting too many customers too far.
He finally went to work in a cotton mill
Downcounty, and rose to be head of their machine shop;
His talent, hitherto untapped, had been
For fixing things. But he died in his 60s.
Father had gone to work to help support
The family after one year of high school.
His first job was night telephone operator,
Then elevator boy at National Life
Insurance Company. There President
DeBoer picked him for a promising young man
And made him clerk under Colonel O.D. Clark,
Secretary, whose private secretary was
Miss Bessie Louella Hight, later my mother.
During my high-school years, Dad was passed over
For promotion. It almost broke his heart.
But finally he could sign himself—too late—
His mental deterioration had set in—
F.W. Hayford, Assistant Secretary.

1985

The Boss's Dog

When the boss's dog attacked my son
I got kind words from everyone.

But when the moment came to act
You'd be surprised how they backtracked:

The minister couldn't get too sore
At such a large contributor,

Nor did the aldermen and mayor
Want to offend the chief taxpayer.

As for the workmen in his shop,
What would they do if that should stop?

And soon the butcher and the baker
Were calling me a trouble-maker:

He was a longtime resident
And I an upstart malcontent—

Until to hear the dialog
You'd think my son attacked the dog.

1973

217

All Hallows Eve

This night of the year reserved
For ghostly occupation,
Prepare to be unnerved
By dread communication.

Tonight the windy yard
Is not our own to govern;
For once we must regard
The powers of hell and heaven.

There is no strength of lock
Nor length of window shade
Will foil the horrid knock
Of the nocturnal raid.

1951

Autumn Scene

Muted and neat our autumn scene
In shades of gray and evergreen:

Litter of leaves swept up and burned,
House buttoned up, garden adjourned,

And hardwoods standing stripped and still—
All neatly naked in the chill.

1963

218

Closed In

Our walls began to rise
Later than most begin,
So we'll lay roofing tin
Until this dark day dies
To get ourselves closed in
Before snow flies.

1985

Builder

Builder, you're only hired
To house the space required
At prices we accept;

Still, you can try for grace,
And maybe that will place
Your name where names are kept.

1967

Our City in the Cloud

How little that we planned
Is actually in hand,
And how absurdly dear
That little, seen from here.

Our city in the cloud
Has failed, and we are proud
If any one of ours
Raises the least of towers.

1952

Models of Greatness

I
The builders of long palaces
And high cathedrals trusted size

To model without using words
The greatness of their given Lords:

Horizontal stood for temporal,
Eternal came out vertical.

II
Our tree is great
Due to the weight
Of age and size—
Size is, in a tree,
What age supplies.

Delay your fate
Till you accumulate
Size to shade half an acre,
And then you too may be
A model of the greatness of your Maker.

1979

Building a House

Having too long made do
With other people's rooms,

Take your chance to renew
Your postponed plans and schemes—

Unless by now your doom's
More comfortable than dreams.

1986

Necessary Bulge

The builder seeking to exclude
All minor infelicities
From public surfaces
May find he has to let protrude
A necessary bulge, high, low,
Or off-side where it won't much show—
A stairwell, say, or storage vault—
And pray it won't be judged a major fault.

1984

Old Walls

As supermarkets and motels
Crowd the old college town
And cause the tearing down
Of fine brick mansions with brick ells,

The college will restore
Its Federal and Colonial halls
And houses—even Civil War—
And thus save some old walls.

1966

Keeping Up Appearances

This photo shows the crack
In the plaster in the hall.
Curator, will you jack
And straighten up that wall
As you ideally ought,
Or just touch up the shot?

1984

221

The Joint

A certain men's room wall
Is framed with strips of wood
Whose corners join, or should,
Inside the toilet stall.

The joint nearest at hand,
However, as I stand,
Is such a careless fit
I stand pondering it

Most every time I visit:
Oh yes, I say, I see
What it's supposed to be,
But it just isn't, is it.

1988

Chartres

Your mismatched towers have long enough defeated
The intended order of your front:
The South tower is the one to be repeated—
The top of North needs South's twin steeple.
As Bishop of Chartres, I
Would feel obliged to be blunt:
No insufficient funds nor hidebound people,
No precedent nor lack of precedent
Shall any more deny
The original builders' clear intent.

1985

Front Door

A little should be made of the front door—
Some special framing or a decoration—
Not too much—rather less than more;

Simply a quiet declaration
To anyone who enters here:
Expect some change of atmosphere.

1985

Doll's House

The doll's house with interior light
Made me in outer dark aspire
To join its resident family
Sleeping and getting meals without
Ever attending school or dying.

1984

Catnap

You with your clean pink nose
Tucked in your folded paws,

You at your morning nap,
You spent the night abroad.

Who's answerable to God
For the dead mouse at the door?

Lord, if you're keeping score,
He functions as my trap.

1951

223

The Jungle in the House

The housecat never lacks
For cozy bivouacs—

A chairseat snugly girt,
Or his protector's skirt.

Yet threats we turn our backs
On, dog the housecat's tracks.

Even in sleep alert
Against approaching hurt,

He cannot quite relax
For fear of—what attacks?

1953

Back the Same Day

Come see how lazily it's snowing.
The wind is scarcely blowing.

The sky is white, the ground is white.
This whiteness, like the black of night,
Makes all things one to sight.

We fall asleep when all is one
And waken in the sun.

By opposites we make our way:
We work and rest, and work and play.
But time is all one day.

We pass from coming into going.
How lazily it's snowing.

1935

Room of Snow

Industriously the weaver Snow
Lets down the thick stuff from his loom
To shimmer past the lamps and shut
The village in a snow-walled room.

1937

Old Man's Firewood

Time enough for one more load,
The old man tells his mare,
And she steps down the road
To the low sawmill where
In early valley dark
He piles slabs on the sleigh:
Sufficient to his need
Has been his winter's day.

1951

Valley Town

In this deep-valley town
Our winter sun will set
By half-past two, or three;

While you can probably
Get where you have to get
Before night quite shuts down,

You haven't got all day.

1975

The Hour in Hand

The hour in hand may prove too scant
To tell how tired I am of time
As told by works that tick and chime,
Or by the light's declining slant,
In units of an hour, a day.
At three I must away

Not to return until this room
Where now I sit in general light
Drifts single on the tide of night
Which sweeps somebody to his doom.
What if not this time me or you?
Someone we know, or knew.

1955

Itinerant Piano Teacher

A snowstorm veiling half Vermont
Wouldn't prevent my Friday jaunt
Downcountry to the county seat
To trade some music for some meat,
And warm myself with local gentry
Meantimes in public room or entry,
Looking at blurry lights and people
And some considerable steeple.

1952

A Profitable Dealing

Some days the heart would fail
From future-fright and loathing
Did not the belly frail
With need of food and clothing

Compel us to maintain
A profitable dealing
With partners of our pain,
Whose patience is our healing.

1951

The Houses in the Town

By day, light shining in
Scarce penetrates their thin
Layer of domestic skin;

By night, light shining out
Admits no room for doubt
Their hearts are warm and stout.

1951

The People in Their Houses

Ignoring the north wind
Which in the street carouses
With me its only friend,
The people in their houses
Secure from search or seizure
By prying hands that pass,
Resort to sleep or pleasure
In barricades of glass.

1966

Out on the Town

As I was rambling round the town—
The streets bend up, the streets bend down,
Composing patchwork views
Of preposterous shapes and hues:
A store on top of a church
Whose spire bisects a porch
That seems to belong to a stable
With a dormer stuck in one gable—
As I was rambling round the town
I met a man who said with a frown,
"The cultural level here is low."

"How so?
Why, there's a library and two museums,
Nine churches to supply Te Deums,
A daily paper,
A linen draper
Who wears stiff collars
And writes to scholars,
A courthouse and jail
And frequent mail,
Northern New England's Largest Garage—"

"Fah! Just because a thing is large—"

"New England's narrowest shoeshine stand,
A park
With a stand for the band
To play summer nights at dark,
Two hospitals and a clinic—"

"Oh whoa and hush, you cynic!"

"Freight yards and factories, complete—
All of a county seat,
A whole provincial capital."

"And oh so cultural!
Come now, you know these people have no goal

Except to bowl
Or see a movie show—
The cultural level, as I said, is low.
Don't boost,
Rotarian; let's knock."

"You mean the band don't render Bach?
The shop-help don't read Proust
And Austen,
Like in Boston?"

"You know what I mean. For shame!"

"You mean folks are to blame
Because they're not the same
As you are. Your fine taste
They call a waste.
What you call fun
They shun.
They're in
What you call sin."

"How'd sin get in?
I just want civilization.
How can you run a nation
If you don't have civilization?"

"I don't seem to be running one.
Haven't the time. Have all I can do to run
Myself. No one I know is such a brute."

"Quit being cute."

"O.K., quit being holy.
What I am learning, slowly,
A man's a man, whether he ever heard of Burns.
No matter what he earns
Or where he turns,
He learns.
One of my main concerns,

Out on the town today,
Is learning what he learns."

"What's this—a café?"

"I forgot it in my résumé.
Come have a quiet cultural drink.
It's earlier than you think."

1952

In the Stable

By rights this factory should close tonight
So that we too could have our holiday,
But you ladies would get too full of milk
If we should skip our evening choretime. So,
Let's get to work as usual, you and I.
Our customers will want their Christmas milk.
We should be glad of their demand and our
Supply—which brings me in not quite enough
To buy you ladies all gold chokers. However,
Maybe you'll take the Christmas thought for the deed.
I *can* put extra molasses on your feed,
And after, fork you out some premium hay.

1984

Snowscape

Mountains the late sun crowns with bronze
Cast blue dusk down our lawns,
Which might be swollen seas
With high snow lapping at the trees.

1966

Winter Business

My business is to be abroad
These brief but brilliant afternoons
When maples, lately green balloons
With inwards private as a pod,

Display that structure slant and odd
Along which robins and raccoons
Conducted wars and honeymoons
In secret between sky and sod.

1951

Winter Day

Because the ground was white
And the cloud almost black,
Sky-light drained down less bright
Than what the snow sent back.

Absence of shadow kept
All the hours the same:
I watched the world and slept,
And watched till darkness came.

1967

Winter Dusk

White hills at sundown show
Sunset and streetlight shine,
Which for a while combine
To dazzle on the snow.

1986

The Scalloped Scene

Out for his solo walk—
To whom was he to talk
About his apprehensions,
Misgivings no one mentions—

He came where new snow sifted
On frozen snow had drifted
In loops and rhythmic scrolls
A meadowful of knolls.

He fixed the scalloped scene
Upon his optic screen,
Wavy-white, ankle-deep,
Till he should try to sleep.

1951

The Watches of the Night

Let him whom sleep eludes
Have drowsy episodes

When all he wants to be
Comes magically true—

And next time he comes to,
It's four instead of three.

1983

The Idea of His Strength

The sun surmounting the eastern shoulder
At twelve, thirteen, fourteen of eight,
When I sit down to breakfast late
I sit in light though the days are colder.

Warmed by the idea of his strength
Which will by noon set eaves adrip,
I celebrate his generalship
By reckoning tomorrow's length.

1951

Still Wintering

They say it's almost spring,
But I'm still wintering—
Still staying used to cold.

I've simply got too old
To lightly shed my coat,
Much less begin to gloat.

1984

Spring Shade

Come spring, in the encircled house benighted
The house-bound one waits undelighted—

Waits for the fall of leaves in autumn,
And snow-light when the round year hits bottom.

1949

Flat Fields

Flat fields that see the sun all day
Are all but bare of snow,
And in the dense dead last-year's hay
New green shoots start to show.

When I was green as those young spears
Sad in the fall I'd sing;
Now that I have good use for tears,
I'm glad to sing in spring.

1959

Egg in the Pocket

Go pocket a fresh egg
And then go bump that leg
Next time you come to turn

A corner in the barn;

Maybe someday you'll learn
What not to leave to chance—
Including nice dry pants.

1950

Choirmaster

Hearing the sweet birds take the sky
On sunny waves of lilac scent,
As local choirmaster I
Would have us follow where they went
And, like them, toss our notes so high
We feel and cause astonishment.

1982

Local Characters

A Local Character

When Grover told me Ben was back in town,
Working for his father in the feed store,
I almost said, Good Lord, what a comedown!
Instead I said, "Oh? What brings him back here?"

"You ought to know. Aren't you the music man?"

Downstairs the printing press slammed to and fro.
The building shook, and Grover's windows rattled.
Framed prints of Pulitzer and Greeley jumped.
(Grover's the editor of our weekly sheet.)

I stalled for time. "He didn't make the grade?"

Grover snorted. "What else is there to think?"

"Nothing, I guess. Who knows how hard he tried—"

"Not hard enough. Maybe I shouldn't talk.
He's good, isn't he? I like to hear him sing.
They tell how Tibbett gave him a kind word."

"He's pretty good," I said.

                              "But not that good—
Not big-league stuff? Couldn't he be if he tried?"

"Who's to say how hard any of us try,
Or what we could be if we really did?"

"Well—" Grover frowned. "You've got me there. I'm not,
Let's say, editor of the *New York Times*."

"I'm not conductor of the Philharmonic."

"You do a fair job with the village choir—
Considering the stuff you've got to work with."

"Thanks. You do fairly well with the *Enterprise*."

"All right! Let's quit cheering each other up."

"I'm not cheered in the least, and neither are you."

"No. I don't know whether to be mad at Ben

237

For giving up, or at the system for
Rejecting him."

        "But anyway, you're mad."

"Yes."

      "So am I, I reckon, in a way.
You hate to see a youngster bruised like that.
But baritones these days are a dime a dozen—
Good ones. So are performers of all sorts.
The cities are chock full of slick performers.
Technical perfection's taken for granted.
Ben isn't slick, nor technically perfect.
He's individual—he's odd, eccentric."

Grover laughed. "He's come to the right place."

"He's come back home," I said.

           "All right. Now what?"

"Well now, let's see. What would we have him do?
He's got his craft—singing, his hero—Tibbett.
(I looked at Grover's Pulitzer and Greeley.)
Let him stay here and please us with his voice—
The choir and our annual cantata—
And settle down and be a character—
Like us, Grover, a local character!"

1954

The Boss's Wife

At last he came down the road; she met him with:

"What kept you?"

        "We were late starting to milk."

"I thought she must be chasing you again."

"Oh, her!"

      "What did she say?"

           "I didn't see her."

"You sure?"

        "Of course I'm sure. You're cold, aren't you?
We better get inside. Too cold tonight
To ripen corn."

          "I thought sure she'd been at you."

"Again? She knows by this time it's no use."

"That's what you think."

           "Why not?"

                "I know her kind."

"Oh Annie! You know so much that isn't so."

"Do I? Who was it said you couldn't trust
Old Murray when he didn't pay you for plowing?
Who was it knew—"

          "All right, all right, you knew.
I'm sorry. Don't be mad. You knew all right."

"You're such a fool."

           "Yes, I suppose I am."

"A nice fool."

          "Well, that helps."

             "You'd rather be
A nice fool that's surprised when he gets hurt."

"Rather be that than what?"

            "A nasty fool
Like me that goes around expecting trouble."

"And often doesn't find it?"

            "Often does.
I tell you, when a woman isn't happy
With her own house and husband, she won't rest
Until she's made somebody else unhappy—
Especially her husband's hired help.
I know these discontented would-be ladies."

239

"I see. But Annie, what can she do to us?"

"Oh, she knows how to ruin happiness."

"Like ours?"

       "Of course. Fred, tell me why you love me."

"You know—"

       "But you don't quite know, do you now,
These last months when I'm clumsy and big in front.
Other women have prettier bodies—"

          "Annie—"

"Excuse me. You love me these days simply because
It somehow seems the thing you ought to do."

"Annie—"

       "And all she has to do is make
You wonder, for one minute, whether, perhaps,
You oughtn't to be doing something else—
She with her smooth, slim, tanned, svelte body—"

          "Stop it!"

"Oh sure, but then you reassure yourself
Of my peculiar charms—lips, hair, and eyes,
Etcetera; the fact that I can cook;
The fact that I am pregnant with your child—"

"Annie, look here, you've got to stop this."

          "No.
I know what happens when you have to think
Whether you ought to be doing what you are.
You need sound reasons, Fred, real reasons, not
Just lips and hair."

       "Perhaps I love you, Annie,
For your sound reason *and* your lips and hair.
Come in, where we can soundly, warmly reason."

1951

240

A Man's Work

In a high field sloping to a valley view
A man and a grown boy raking sparse hay.

"Dad, what's the use? This stuff isn't worth the trouble."

"You mean just leave it here and let it rot?"

"It wouldn't hurt the field—it might manure it."

"But we need hay—we can't afford to buy it."

"Look, if we went and caddied at the club
We could earn more this afternoon, with luck,
Than what this measly rained-on hay is worth."

"You go if you want. That isn't a man's work."

"You call this working for nothing a man's work?"

"It isn't for nothing, son. It isn't much,
But it's not nothing. We'll get a fair load."

"Enough to feed the cattle say a week."

"A week's a week."

                    "And that leaves fifty-one.
Dad, can't you see you just aren't going to make it?"

"I've made it so far, one way or another.
It wouldn't be right to leave it here to rot.
Go if you want. I'll get it in alone."

"Someday I'm going to leave *you* here to rot—
But not today. All right, let's get it in."

1957

241

Socks for Mr. Barnes

"Ma! Fancy meeting you in Woolworth's!"

                          "Hello."

"What are you, doing your Christmas shopping early?"

"No, I came in for socks for Mr. Barnes."

"So now you're buying Barnes's socks! Well, well."

"With Mr. Barnes's money, May."

                        "Of course.
You're just his housekeeper, of course."

                         "Of course."

"You keep your money separate from his,
He keeps his red nose out of your affairs.
Oh, everything's so nice and separate!
He has his bed and you have yours, and—"

                         "May!"

"Say, tell me, how do you ever stand his smell—
Stale sweat, stale beer, tobacco—and that cough—
Hack, hawk—why, that would drive me out of my head.
One reason I got through with men—the smells,
The coughs. I don't see how you stand it, ma,
You used to be so dainty."

                    "May! Shut up!"

"But things were different then. You had a home
Of your own, and a man, not rich but decent—
Don't pa ever haunt you, sometimes, nights, when you and—"

"Keep your tongue off your father! You don't know
Even how to talk about a decent man."

"Oh no? And if I don't, whose fault is that?
After the way you lied about me to George—"

"If any lying was done to George Bessette,
I know who did it—you, you awful *woman!*"

1952

242

Light-Minded Dame

Evelyn S. Lease 1866-1957

Come in. Give me a minute and I'll name you—
Of course—how are you, James? It's been some years.
Don't be alarmed—my mind is pretty good;
It's slow, that's all—it likes to take its time.
You're getting bald, too, aren't you? Never mind.
Why are we so surprised when young friends age?
Well now, you'll eat a piece of gingerbread?
I made myself some gingerbread and cream,
Just for a treat. The appetite's one sense
That doesn't fail. I heard Dr. Eliot—
You know, forever President of Harvard—
At a librarians' convention tell
Of calling on an aged dame who might,
He hoped, be led to say a weighty thing
About the meaning of life. He asked her what
As she looked back had meant the most to her.
"My vittles," she replied. Second the motion.
Here. Oh, you'll want a spoon. So 'tis you find me,
Devising treats and wasting time I ought
To spend on cramming for my finals—ha!
(You know: Why's Grandma always reading her Bible?
Well, son, I guess she's cramming for her finals.)
But come—look here—the funeral home, remember?
As a rule I see it from this back window.
See there, it's almost hidden by the snowbank.
That must account for my light-mindedness.

1952

243

The Judge's Wife

"I just saw Burton Fairfax and his wife."

"Where?"

    "Oh, downtown."

        "She wasn't bringing him here?"

"No, he was squiring her around the stores,
She on his arm, he looking proud as Punch.
Let me stir that—or shall I set the table?
He is a handsome man, poor man."

            "Poor man!"

"If he hadn't been so vain she wouldn't have got him—
The little tittering, painted, ancient thing.
Remember how he wouldn't even look
At you when you two were in school together?
I hated him for slighting my young sister."

"I lived. I've hardly seen him since. So there.
Besides, I'm nearly as ancient as she is.
Didn't she come from over Danville way?"

"North Danville. Nothing local was good enough.
Pshaw! Nothing local would play up to him."

"I might have, given a chance. But how's he doing,
As judge? You wrote me he was elected judge
Of county court."

            "Oh, very well, I guess.
They sold the farm and bought that great big house—
The Porter place—not far from the courthouse.
She had enjoyed poor health for years, you know—
Till Burton was made judge. Then she picked up.
She told folks she would have to entertain
A good deal now that Burton was a judge."

"Some of you found that prospect entertaining."

"There was some talk that Burton would divorce her."

"So? On account of whom?"

                        "A woman lawyer
Who's come to town from down Massachusetts way,
Forty or so, and smart, and he admires her.
She dabbles some in local politics.
Hold this—I want to look in at the roast."

"Well?"

             "Well, for a while it looked as if he might.
They lunched together and left the courthouse late
Together."

        "Ah!"

             "So everybody said."

"You couldn't have blamed him very much, could you?
So nothing came of it?"

               "No."

                  "He fooled you all.
He proved he was a judge, with too much judgment
To fall for an ambitious spinster lawyer."

"That doesn't make him a hero. Lord, what's left
Between him and that silly wife of his?"

"What was there ever there? Come now, be fair.
It's touching to see how courtly he's become
Toward his poor silly wife. He takes her arm
To help her out of the car into a store,
And listens with impassive gravity
While she convicts herself, with witnesses."

1952

245

A Wild One

"Herb Morrison's a friend of yours."

                      "Sure. Why?"

"He's been on a bat for two weeks."

                      "So I hear—
Ever since Irene died. He took it hard.
I had an idea he would."

                  "Were they married?"

"I don't know. I guess so. He never said.
Whatever the arrangement was, it worked.
She was a wild one too. They both had their
Opinions of polite society."

"Well, the factory phoned. If Herb's not back
By Monday morning they don't want him back—
He's through."

      "So?"

                "So he'll end up on the town.
We don't propose to have him on the town."

"Who's we? Oh, you're a selectman—I forget.
I don't believe I'd worry about that.
I doubt if Herb would take your charity."

"Oh? Let's not give him the chance."

                    "Now listen, Dave.
I doubt if Herb would listen to advice
From me, or even you. He's independent."

"Where did he blow from into here?"

                      "Boston,
I think. I never did get all his story.
He comes from a good family—that is, good
As we would say—maybe not good for him.
His father was an architect, well known.
Herb's done all sorts of work—been on the road,
Kept store—all over the United States,

246

Strictly on his own terms. He never got caught.
He likes to tell of times when he rebelled
And knocked somebody down that tried to run him.
Drink isn't what has kept him on the loose.
I don't know how much Herb trusts me—I talk
A good rebellion but I don't rebel."

"Do you trust him?"

                          "As a friend, yes, perfectly.
As a fellow-citizen—I see your point.
He isn't what we'd call community-minded.
We got acquainted through both keeping goats;
We borrowed the same buck to breed our does.
Goats are a fraternal bond in cow country.
Another goat keeper, not Herb, asked me
If I had noticed there was something odd
About all the goat people I had met.
He was a character all right himself.
I read something funny in a goat book once.
It said goats are such gentle characters
The good goat man must be a gentle man . . .
I thought you'd find that funny. Irene knew:
Herb took her in when that drunk she lived with
Had thrown her out. That little place of theirs
With the house Herb built from odds and ends of boards
Was a refuge for abandoned animals—
Dogs, cats, a baby skunk, a wounded crow,
And so many goats they had to hang them up—
They couldn't bear to part with the useless ones.
Who's caring for the stock—oh, Herb, how are you?"

"I've been better. I'm caring for the stock—
As you could have found out by coming up.
They're Irene's pets—she'd haunt me if I didn't."

"I'm sorry, Herb. I didn't come because
I didn't think you'd want folks underfoot."

"I got drunk, and I've stayed drunk ever since."

"Yuh. Look here, Herb, the factory just phoned—"

"They did! Well, well. Well, they can go to hell."

"They want you back by Monday—"

                             "And so can you.
What are you, Dave, scared I'll go on the town?
What is this, Ralph—you two deciding what
You're going to do with me?"

                      "Now listen, Herb—"

"Ralph, are you in on this?"

                    "I just told Dave
I didn't think you'd want to be advised."

"You said you saw my point—"

                   "What point, Ralph, pal?"

"You know Dave's a selectman, Herb. He's got
Official worries about the taxpayers' cash."

"O.K., you worry about it, boys. So long."

"Well, what about your drunken friend now, Ralph?"

"My drunken friend is still my friend—if he
Forgives my listening to your taxpayer-talk
While he was in his misery."

                 "Look, Ralph,
I have to talk taxpayer-talk."

                "Sure, Dave.
With Irene gone, he'll hit the road again."

"You sure?"

            "I wouldn't worry about Herb."

1956

The Over-Praised Wife

Cliff ain't just right in the head, you know what I mean.
You have to look after him like a little child.
He wasn't always that way—wasn't so bad
When we got married, but since his accident . . .
Tractor threw him and ran right over his head.
Oh, I ain't claiming he was no A-student
Before—I knew that when I married him.
Everybody said they was sorry for me
Back then before he had his accident.
But he was steady—had a good farm started—
Hard worker—and he was always good to me.
It wasn't hard at all to be patient with him.
He never could figure—you know, interest money
Or government taxes, or how much six dozen eggs
Should fetch at forty cents. I know my timeses
Up to seven times twelve, and figure the rest
By adding. I done all the farm figuring,
And read him the paper, when we had the time,
And everybody said how good I was to him.
But it wasn't hard back then to *be* good to him.
He maybe was better than most at some bed-games.
He wasn't never mean or ugly. Now
You never know. Some days he's meek as Moses,
Just like before, but other days, look out.
Don't let him get his hands on you. He's strong,
Still strong; he always was, and he still is.
I've got the scars to show you, mister. Look.
He jumped me just this afternoon, about five,
When I got back from cashing the welfare check
And picking up our food stamps for the month.
I finally talked him into taking a pill,
And fixed his supper, and wheeled him out back here.
And you drove by and saw me digging the garden
Behind the trailer, and him asleep in his chair,
And you said to yourself, "Now there's a picture!
Devoted wife slaving for crippled husband.
The world's still safe—especially Vermont."
Not what you thought? Well, almost. Strangers do.

You just ask any of the neighbors, though.
They'll tell you I'm a double dirty whore.
Remember what I told you they used to say—
How extra good I was to foolish Cliff?
Well, now he's mean and ugly half the time,
And you never know which half, I've got a boyfriend.
He's due about now. He drops in every night
Soon as he sees I've got Cliff put to sleep.
Just stick around. You'd probably like to meet him.
It might round out your picture—where you going?
Look, I didn't ask for *praise*—oh, go to hell.

1970

Running for Bishop

"Parson, would you consider running for Bishop?"

"Me? Bishop? Henry, you don't 'run' for Bishop!"

"I put it crudely—no offense intended.
I just meant, would you let your name be raised—
Let it be known that you're available?"

"Available? You mean ambitious, don't you?"

"No. You know how it is. Given two men,
One known to be—well, call it not averse,
The other not known, other things being equal,
The Convention is inclined to choose the first;
They have to reconvene if their choice reneges.
You say the word and we'll put your name up."

"Oh, I wouldn't have a chance against—never mind.
That's not the point. I lack the qualifications."

"Isn't that for the Convention to decide?"

"Well—yes. But if I let you raise my name,
It would appear I think I'm qualified."

"No, George. You'd just be saying you wouldn't refuse.
You know, of course, who certainly *won't* refuse—
You almost said his name a minute ago—"

"You mean—"

        "I mean our popular Dean Sinclair.
He certainly thinks he has the inside track."

"Can you see him as Bishop?"

               "No, can you?"

"My candidate would be our friend Sylvester."

"Not Saint Sylvester! Come, George, he couldn't win."

"Too spiritual, you think?"

            "Ethereal, George.
What we need is a good practical Bishop."

"Practical, eh? That's Dean Sinclair all over."

"Too practical. That's what they say, honest.
I've done some canvassing. Political
Is what they call Sinclair. You're popular
Around the diocese—in a good way.
Respected popular. You're listened to.
You're saintly *and* you're practical—you're both."

"Henry, Henry—you've been telling them *that?*"

"I thought you wanted to be Bishop, George.
I thought that was the ambition of all priests—
The way I want to be President of the Company."

"There's a difference, Henry, in these offices:
A President needs only competence—
He doesn't have to be a practical saint."

"How about a fighter hankering to be champ?"

"Champs have a chance to win in a fair fight.
Besides, their business is to be ambitious—
Their nature is ambitious, and that's good.
It isn't politics that gets them there."

"I'm not suggesting you play politics!"

"What it boils down to is, if I don't take it
Somebody else will, who might be worse than me."

"No, you're the strongest of three qualified men."

"Ambitious shepherds! Politicking pastors—
You know what Milton thought of them: 'Blind mouths!'
'Blind mouths! that scarce themselves know how to hold
A sheep-hook, or have learn'd aught else the least
That to the faithful herdsman's art belongs!
The hungry sheep look up, and are not fed . . .'
I shouldn't talk this way about bishops, though.
We've had fine bishops in this diocese—
Hall, Booth, Van Dyck, and Butterfield—
Those four go back nearly a hundred years.
All spiritual men, all humble men—and yet,

252

As you are going to remind me—yet
Sufficiently ambitious not to refuse.
But why throw good men in the way of this
Temptation to be proud? The Bishop—ah!
You said it, he's the champ, the chosen one.
The fact that he works harder, travels further,
And has more worries than the rest of us,
That's all offset by his unique prestige.
Who thinks of headaches when he sees the Bishop,
The Bishop in his purple, with his cross,
The Bishop with his chaplain in his chapel—
Would Jesus feel at home in the Bishop's House—
Not that Rock Point is that palatial,
Though it is fancier than this rectory.
You see why I say I am not the man—
I can't withstand temptation to be proud.''

"Too proud, George, of not being proud?''

                                "Now wait—
That hurt. The sin against the Holy Ghost?
It takes so many forms you never know—''

"What makes you think Hall, Booth, and Butterfield
Didn't ask themselves the same disturbing questions?''

"Well—they were men—''

                    "And lively men, like you.
I'd say it ought to make things easier.
You'd be at the top—you wouldn't have to fear
Ambition any more, or failure either.
The love of God that would well up in you,
And would be answered from the other side—''

"If chosen, I would *gain* the qualifications?''

"I'm betting on it, George.''

                        "All right, I'll run.''

1957

253

The Start of Something

"Dave, why'd you call me for a date?"

                              "I like you."

"You hardly know me."

                    "I'd like to know you better."

"I shouldn't find much fault with that, should I?
What *am* I doing?"

              "Same thing as me, I guess—
Thinking this might be the start of something."

"Yes—Dave, what do we want it to be?"

                                   "A friendship?
Well, there's nothing wrong with friendship, is there?
Even some married couples—"

                    "Still stay friends?
Dave, don't be funny. Let's be serious."

"It's easier to be funny, but you're right."

"You're basically a serious fellow, aren't you?"

"You're certainly a serious girl. I'm glad."

"Are you? I was afraid you wouldn't be.
What you said about married couples then—"

"But I was being funny—"

              "No, you weren't—
Not wholly—I didn't see it then—"

                         "See what?"

"It's kind of sadly true."

              "And funnily?"

"Yes."

         "There you are, you see. The sad is funny,

The funny is sad."

"What *is* the use of talk?"

"Oh, lots of use. What else is there but talk?"

"Well—"

"Sex, you mean?"

"David, I didn't say it."

"I see that. You invited me to say it."

"All right, you said it."

"I told you all was talk.
Even sex is talk—before, during, and after."

"Sure, making love is talking—"

"Talking is making—"

"*That's* what we're doing!"

"You like it all right so far?"

"I like it fine. But mother never told me—"

"Now who's being funny?"

"Oh, Dave, I'm sorry—"

"Don't be. We've reached our first agreement—sort of."

1969

255

Miss Cleghorn's Dinner

Sarah N. Cleghorn 1876–1959

"I've come by bus from Philadelphia,"
Miss Cleghorn said when I met her by the store
In Manchester one hot May afternoon.
"After I paid my fare I had ten cents.
I bought an ice cream cone in New York City.
That was five cents, so I have five cents left.
Do you think Mr. Wiley would let me have an egg
For five cents? If he'd give me a paper cup
I'd go across there in the shade and drink it.
There's a nice spot on the bank there by those bushes.
Raw egg is cool, and very nourishing."
She handed me a nickel: "Would you mind—?"
Mr. Wiley sold me an egg and a paper cup.
I was on foot and overdue somewhere,
So I got her and her bag across the road,
Called her a taxi, and left her in the shade.

1952

A Useful Death

Yes, I do know this house needs paint, and no,
I don't intend to paint it. Don't intend
To sell it either, not while I'm alive.
I presume you need a place, but so don't I.
You can have it when I'm gone, for all of me.
Of course there'll be an heir, but he won't want it.
He lives in Omaha, comes once a year.
He's what I'm saving for—he'll be a rich man.
He's had to live poor all his life, poor boy.
Just never had the meanness to get rich.
Some folks might say the gumption, but I don't.
Never mind all that, he can retire rich.
You see, my husband bought four hundred acres
Of woodlot on the mountain years ago.
We were, you might say, land-poor all our lives.
Taxes kept going up, but we hung on.
Then just before he died the skiing people
Needed that land for their expansion scheme.
They gave us eighty-five thousand dollars for it.
Interest on eighty-five thousand dollars—well,
If I last one more year, it'll be a hundred—
A hundred thousand dollars to pass on.
I've worked hard all my life, and gone without,
So I could help my husband and my son—
Helped the whole neighborhood from time to time.
Served one term in the legislature once.
I tried to make my life a useful thing.
Maybe my death'll be of some use, too.

1970

257

The Interviewer

"What do you want?"

                "To ask you how you do."

"Pretty fair, thank you. That all?"

                      "How do you live?"

"How do I live! Like anybody else."

"What—in this shed abutted by two barns
On the main street of a dying village?"

                          "Sure.
Somebody's got to live here, haven't they?
At least, I've got to live somewhere, haven't I?
Who are you?"

                "A writer. Who are you?"

                        "A man.
How do *you* live?"

                "By asking others that."

"What kind of answers do you get, in general?"

"Not very satisfactory, in general."

"They don't know?"

                "Most of them don't, that's right."

"Come in, sit down. Why don't they, do you think?"

"You like it sort of dark, I take it."

                      "Oh,
My geraniums do fill the windows, don't they?
I seem to think they need more light than I do.
I get enough; I'm out most every day."

"Where do you go?"

                "To the store, to get my mail,
If any. And buy my groceries."

                "Newspaper?"

"No, if the world improves, I'll hear about it.
You want a cup of tea?"

     "That might be good."

"We'll have to wait till the kettle boils. Tell me,
Does everybody give you tea, or coffee?"

"You mean do they like my butting in. Some do.
Some think I'm spying for their creditors
Or the police or the government."

       "You're not—?"

"Pure curiosity."

    "How the other half live?"

"No, I wouldn't know which half I should be classed with."

"I see. Well, in the winter I sleep a lot,
In bed, in there, in order to keep warm.
I hibernate, some of the neighbors say.
This shed stays awful cold, best I can do."

"Look out the windows some?"

       "Oh yes, good days
When the sun pours in. I keep a hole pruned through
Between these two plants by my rocker here—
See—I can see who's passing in the road
Without their seeing me. You've passed here often?"

"Quite often."

     "And never saw me, before today.
I sit in the dark and look out nights, when it's warm.
My wife died thirteen years ago."

       "Lonesome?"

"Sometimes. I try not to make a virtue of it.
I bet I'm not much lonesomer than you.
I chose to move in here because it's cheap."

"What do you think about?"

      "What I did today,
And what I'll do, and have to eat, tomorrow.

Oh! The kettle's hot. I'll make the tea.
I do something each day—like wash a shirt
Or fix the weatherstripping round the door.
Gives me something to do, and plan to do,
And be satisfied with having done.
You take it with milk, or sugar?"

                                   "I like it straight."

"Good, so do I. Now what about *your* life?
How satisfactory do you think *you* are?"

1969

Innocent Passage

"Father, your suffering makes me doubt God."

"I suffer nothing but what can be borne.
Why can't you bear to let me bear it, son?"

"I feel I ought to bear it for or with you."

"That's generous—I thank you—but quite false."

"It's not much use, I guess, but false—why false?"

"Because the universe is innocent
And our ordeal is part of its order.
If it becomes too hard we rave or die.
Compassion is complicity against God.
Get me a glass of water and go your way."

1955

260

Why She Stayed

Toward noon he spoke of it again: "Daughter,
Why don't you go—why don't you marry him?"

The two of them were cutting pulp in the swamp
At the far end of the farm. The sun was hot;
Despite the flies, they'd shed the woolen shirts
They wore coming out in the misty morning.

For answer, she impatiently shook her head.

Slowly he straightened up, laid down his ax,
Glanced at the sun. "You ready for your dinner?"

Again she shook her head, bending more deeply
Over the new-felled cedar she was trimming.

"You want to work a while more?"

       "I can't eat."

"You mustn't work without eating. Want to go home?"

"No, I'm all right."

     "You may get hungry later.
Let's work a while more." He picked up his ax,
Then laid it down again. "Cassie," he said,
" I don't intend to boss. You'll do as you like.
I'm puzzled, that's all. Why don't you want to go?
Why don't you want to marry?"

       "I don't know."

"Don't you like Charley Burgess?"

        "Yes—"

         "Then why—"

"I want to stay with you."

      "Why, bless your heart.
I'm glad to have you—you know that."

        "I'll stay."

"But Cassie, look, there's other things to think of.
Don't you want your own home? Don't you want children?"

"Isn't this my own home?"

                    "And I'm your child?
In a way, I am. You have looked after me
Since you were twelve and Mother died of the flu.
You've done a woman's work since you were twelve."

"This isn't woman's work!" With a flourish she
Clipped off the final branch.

                    "No, and I hate—"

"I like it! Don't you see, Pa? Charley doesn't.
He thinks you abuse me. He won't say so, but
That's what he thinks."

                    "Charley thinks that?"

                          "Yes, Pa.
He says he won't have me out in the woods,
Or even in the barn. That's what he says.
A woman's work, he says, is in the house—
Dishes and cooking, sewing, making beds—"

"Well, Charley's right, of course."

                    "Oh Pa!"

                    "In the main.
If it wasn't for my wounded knee—"

                    "That's it,
That's it—you need me, see? That's the whole point."

"No, daughter, that is not the point. The point
Is you, not me. What future is there for you
In nursing me along for a few years?
You won't have any clothes—look at you, dressed
In old patched pants and shirt like—well, like me!
You won't have a nice house with electric lights,
You won't have any fun—"

                    "I'll make us bowls
Of popcorn over the kitchen fire at night,
Now won't I, Pa?"

                "Yes, Cassie, I'm sure you will."

"All right. Now where'd you put the lunch? Oh, here.
What do you want first, egg or tomato sandwich?"

"Egg. I'm not hungry now. Cassie, I wonder—"

"What do you wonder, Pa?"

                              "You've had so little,
I wonder if you don't mistrust good luck."

"Why Pa, my luck is wonderful! Here, eat."

So Cassie stayed and did her woman's work,
And turned into the toothless, furtive creature
Occasional visitors to her crippled father
Spy peeking through the doorway-crack today.

And so the folks down in the village say,
"He worked the poor girl till she lost her mind."

1953

Silas, the Ideal King

A man discovered in a shack in the woods.
Enter to him another man, who speaks:

"I saw where someone spat tobacco juice
In the snow beside my path. So it was you."

"No one ever comes here?"

                            "Almost no one."

"Just about what I thought. I thought at first
I'd cover it up. But then I figured no,
I'd leave it for a warning."

                      "Warning eh?
So I could flee? So I could run away?"

"So you could prepare yourself."

                       "I'm prepared.
You're here. I am unarmed."

                   "I saw to that."

"You've got my rifle?"

                 "No, but neither have you."

"It's gone. What do you mean?"

                     "I threw it out,
In the deep snow. It's safe enough till spring.
I took my chances. You might have been here.
You might have shot me coming up the path.
You weren't. You didn't. That was only luck."

"You don't want luck to play any part in this.
You've got to do this thing all on your own."

"That's right. What are you teetering there for?
Come away from the door! Or maybe it's the window
You're hoping to get out. Or can you be
Expecting help? Are you expecting someone?
Come on!"

"I told you no one ever comes."

"On orders, eh? You leave commands no one
Is to disturb you. This is your retreat
From kingly cares and stress of government.
In that case, do come in, Your Majesty,
And take a seat in your own lodge, or shack,
Or whatever it is you call this quaint
Unfinished and almost unfurnished place."

"Unregal am I? You catch me off guard—
Both literal and figurative. That rifle—
I was all out of shells for it, as you
No doubt discovered. I don't keep much guard."

"You think you're safe in being popular."

"I think I'm safe enough. I really don't know
About the popular. I'd rather be just."

"Squash!"

   "You're the only citizen I know of
With such a grudge against me."

       "What you mean
Is I'm the only one you haven't been
Able to buy, or charm the wits out of.
Oh, I know what the histories will say—
I'll help them write some history today—
Hm—Silas was a good king, as it happened.
Also intelligent. Virtue and brains
Were seldom so mingled in one package.
Whether he could have won in an election—
No, he lacked the evangelistic spirit.
He would have hesitated to impose
Himself on the people under the pretense
That he was God's choice, or the people's choice.
He got to be king by the usual route—
By being first son of a king who died.
Finding himself the king, he set to work—
What are you doing?"

      "Putting wood in the stove.

Here, help me. Hold this miserable door."

"Is it hot?"

        "Yes, here's a kitchen holder. There."

"I could push you in."

           "How messy that would be."

"Well, finding himself king—are you most through?"

"Yes, aren't you?"

        "What do you do here all alone?"

"I come here when I get confused, and books
Are the only voices that I want to hear—
One at a time. How did you find me here?"

"How did I find you? Lord, don't make me laugh."

"I thought you'd be along one of these days.
I only asked from curiosity.
The details of a search are interesting."

"I'll finish now. As king, he set to work
To be as bright and upright as he could.
He read a lot to gather information,
Talked with all kinds of folks to get opinions,
And did his best not to confuse the two.
When he had made up his mind what to do
He told the people what was going to happen
And why he had decided as he had.
He kept reminding them that, as they knew
From making private choices, an advantage
Always carries a built-in disadvantage.
Whenever any citizen was hurt
By any course he took as king, he tried
To make adjustments, often in the form
Of a personal gift or loan. For instance, me.
On one of his tours of mercy he found me
Severely pinched, and gave me—quite a sum."

"That needn't have embittered you. You could,

266

Later, have given it back."

"I'm going to,
Right now, with compound complex interest!
Sit down!"

"You're going to give yourself heart-failure.
You're quite a complex man. It isn't that
You're jealous of what came to me by chance,
And what has cost me mostly work and care.
You wouldn't want to be king—few smart men would,
And fewer still could give adequate reason.
Desire to boss is not much of a reason.
Besides, I don't boss; I'm the public drudge."

"The public what? Why man, wherever you go
People make way for you and whisper, Look,
The King! The King is here! Now we'll hear something!"

"They're really glad to see me, do you think?"

"Of course. They see just you—not what you stand for."

"The principle of rule is what you hate,
The principle that one man should decide
Between conflicting certainties, both right.
But folks still need to know there's one cool head
Deciding. I wish there were one cool head
Over the world—king, president, premier—
But, here you are, intent on doing murder.
I knew you'd be along one of these days."

"You did?"

"There's always one who can't stand peace,
One enemy of settled law and order.
You are the man against whom any state
Must be most watchful to safeguard itself.
Why can't you go live in the woods by yourself,
As I do when I feel at odds with the world?
I'd guarantee to let you right alone."

"Oh no, you can't get rid of me that way.

I won't be bought."

     "No one's trying to buy you.
Could you, or would you, say just what you want?
What do you aim to do by killing me?
Perhaps it's not my business. And perhaps
It is."

   "I hate a hypocrite, you king.
You're not better than the rest of us."

"I never thought I was."

     "Then why be king?"

"I thought I had it in me to be cool,
And fair, and even kind, in a public way.
I thought people needed that kind of king.
I'm going to have a cup of tea."

     "Oh no.
Now what'll become of all your fair ideas?
Put down that chair. Where are you backing to?"

"My body says you'll have hard work to kill it."

"You won't get out of here. There's no other door.
God, help me rid the world of this false thing—
Oh—ow—get me a glass of water."

     "Your heart?"

"Must be. Too much excitement. Oh! Good-bye."

"Good-bye. I'm somewhat sorry you couldn't have won."

"There! Now I've got you, hypocrite and fool!
Leave it to you to be undone by mercy!"

"I may be a fool, but you're the hypocrite.
Now if you win, you'll win the very way
You claim to hate. I'll roll you on your back!
There! Uff! Now—there! You made me mad, you fool."

"Ow! Oh, please get your hands out of my neck."

"Why should I let you live to trick me again?
No, no. You have abused my mercy twice."

"Seventy times seven, the Bible says."

"But you're against mercy, on principle."

"I was. My principles—are changing—fast."

"Get up. Get out. Go live in the woods. Good-bye."

"Good-bye—where are my gloves—long live the King!"

1953

Will You Be Here?

She'd run off with him to a shack in the woods
In winter—one tar-paper-covered room,
One window and a door, a stove, a bed.
Folks in the village couldn't understand
Why in the world she'd left her upstairs rent
With new linoleums, white sink, oil range,
For such a life as this. The man she'd left,
Her husband, was a quiet, steady sort,
Son to the man who owned the lumber mill,
And would no doubt own it someday himself;
This other, a boy still wet behind the ears,
Still talking big of what he meant to do.

The husband took it to the minister
For help. They drove in to the end of the logging road,
Then waded in to the shack through knee-deep snow.
"Good Lord!" the husband said, "Good Lord Almighty!"
The tin-pipe chimney sent a little smoke
Into the hemlock boughs. The pair were at home.
The minister said they'd like to talk with her—
Alone. The boy, leaving, paused and turned
To her: "Will you be here when I come back?"

1937

A Body in the Fog

Warren W. Hartwell 1869–1956

I drove my hearse—that is, I call it a hearse—
A panel truck is what it really is—
I drove from Barton over to Westmore village,
And Albert Gates met me right there by the church
With a pung sleigh to drive up and fetch the body.
Middle of the winter, but there'd been a thaw,
Mild, with some rain—the snow in the road was soft.
You know that road up the hill there by the church—steep.
I noticed, going up, every time the horse
Leaned into it pretty good, Albert pulled back
Hard on the reins to ease him into his collar.
"I dunno," he said, "whether this harness'll stand it.
I patched 'er best I could before I come.
Some odds and ends I had around the barn.
Maybe she'll hold together, maybe she won't."
Well, we got up there all right, and Freeman and I—
I'd brought Freeman along to help—we got
Little Jimmy into my basket and onto the pung.
He was a little Irishman was Jimmy,
Took sick about noon and died in a couple hours.
They sent for me to do him up. He'd come
To this country when he was about fifteen
And settled up in Westmore on that farm,
Nice farm. They guessed his age at eighty-five.
We got him loaded in and started back down.
Well sir, the first little water-bar we came to,
The horse gave a heave and walked right out of his harness.
"There," Albert said. "I'll have to go down to the Gove place
And see what I can borrow for harness gear."
"You take your horse along," I says, "and fix
The whole concern at once and bring him back."
So off he went. By now 'twas really dark,
And foggy, say! That floating, flapping stuff
That sails around in scuds in a thawing spell.
And there we were, stuck off on that hill with a body.
"He'll be an hour," I said to Freeman, "at least.

270

Let's see if you and I can't free this pung."
We'd nosed smack into a bank of snow. You know
How Freeman's built—there ain't a wider man
In the whole state of Vermont. I told him, "Freeman,
You get between the thills"—he filled 'em, too.
I got behind and pulled careful on the basket
And we backed her up a little and got her loose.
Off we went down the hill with Freeman drawing.
I tell you it was a gloomy night to be out in,
With all that creeping fog, even with no body.
We hadn't gone very far when we commenced
To see flashes of dancing light all round,
In with these scuds of fog. My hair rose up,
And so did Freeman's. We stopped and got closer together.
"It's Jimmy," I whispered, "it's Jimmy doing that."
I thought his soul might not care much for the way
We were handling his body—or something might not care—
He was an Irishman . . . After a minute
I said, "Let's get him out of here," and we
Went back to moving the sleigh, holding our breath.
Well, we got down to Gove's—you know what it was?
Albert was out in the yard there at the Gove place
Working on the harness with a lantern
That had a hole in the chimney big as this cup.
That lamp-flame was a-flickering all over,
And being reflected off those scuds of fog.
He got the harness mended and we hitched up.
Gove offered to let us take the lantern. "No,"
I said. "You keep the miserable guttering thing.
We'll be a good deal better off in the dark."

1952

271

Index

273

279

280